WHAT OTHER TEACHERS WON'T TELL YOU:

A Parent's Guide to Coping With School

by

Donald Goodsell

Copyright 2013 by Donald F. Goodsell

1 2 3 4 5 6 7 8 9 10

Why I Wrote the Book

I'm concerned about my two young granddaughter's education. I've spent a lifetime in education, and I want to be sure that when I'm gone their parents (and you) will have a reference to what I have learned and discerned.

Why You Should Read the Book

There are defects in the American education system that the "powers-that-be" choose to ignore. You should know about them, and be prepared to deal with them. There are pertinent questions to be asked and effective actions to be taken as you interact with your children, their teachers, principals, the superintendent, and school board members. Topics include:

- School safety, from bullies to killers
- Indicators of effective classrooms
- Indicators of defective classrooms and how to deal with them
- Improving your child's test scores
- How students can learn the neglected basics
- Students and teachers being robbed of needed class time
- Dealing with inappropriate curriculum.

If you have a crisis of the moment you can use the expanded Table of Contents to go directly to that issue.

Contents

CHAPTER 1 1

SAFETY IN YOUR CHILD'S SCHOOL 1

    YOU AND YOUR CHILD 2

    DEALING WITH THOSE PEOPLE IN SCHOOL 4

    YOU AND YOUR COMMUNITY 12

CHAPTER 2 18

EFFECTIVE AND DEFECTIVE CLASSROOMS 18

    A CLOSE LOOK AT CLASSROOM ATMOSPHERE 20

    CHARACTERISTICS OF GOOD CLASSROOM TEACHING 25

    REVISITING THE EDUCATION CHAIN OF COMMAND 29

CHAPTER 3 31

TESTS: HOW THEY SHOULD BE USED AND HOW TO IMPROVE SCORES 31

    ABOUT STANDARDIZED TESTS 31

    HOW YOU CAN USE YOUR CHILD'S STANDARDIZED TEST SCORES 35

    CLASSROOM GRADING 35

    THE TEACHER AND CLASSROOM TESTS 39

    STUDENT PREPARATION FOR TESTS 40

TEST DAY STRATEGIES	42
COLLEGE ENTRANCE TESTS	44
CHAPTER 4	**49**
LEARNING THE NEGLECTED BASICS	**49**
THE DEMEANING OF ARITHMETIC	49
CALCULATORS	54
CALCULATORS VS SPELLING MACHINES	55
SCIENTIFIC CALCULATORS	56
"WHY JOHNNY CAN'T READ"	56
PHONICS	57
CHAPTER 5	**59**
INAPPROPRIATE CURRICULUM	**59**
COMMON CORE STATE STANDARDS	59
COMMON CORE MATH	60
SHOULD EVERYONE BE A MATHEMATICIAN?	64
COMMON CORE LITERATURE	65
CULTURAL CURRICULUM	66
SEX EDUCATION	67
DRUG EDUCATION	68

BAD PSYCHOLOGY VS GOOD PSYCHOLOGY 70

ENGLISH IS THE MOST IMPORTANT SUBJECT 71

BILINGUAL EDUCATION 72

MULTICULTURALISM 73

CHILD CENTERED SCHOOLS 74

HOMOGENEOUS VS HETEROGENEOUS GROUPING 75

CURRICULUM COORDINATORS 76

TEXTBOOKS 78

VOCATIONAL CURRICULUM 79

ADVANCEMENT 81

CHAPTER 6 83

ROBBING STUDENTS AND TEACHERS OF NEEDED CLASS TIME
.... 83

ELEMENTARY INTERRUPTIONS 83

SECONDARY INTERRUPTIONS 85

TRIPS 89

ATHLETICS 90

TEACHER LESSON PLANS 92

STUDY HALLS 93

HOMEROOM 94

- CAFETERIA DUTY 96
- A HOST OF OTHER ACTIVITIES 96
- SETTING PRIORITIES 97

CHAPTER 7 99

BEWARE OF EDUCATION INNOVATION 99

- TRADITIONAL CLASSROOM VS GROUP STUDY 99
- COOPERATIVE LEARNING 101
- LEARNING STYLES 102
- MASTERY TEACHING 102
- OUTCOME BASED EDUCATION 103
- WHAT DO TEACHERS REALLY THINK? 105
- TECHNOLOGY AND EDUCATION 106
- CLASS SIZE 108
- THE OPEN CLASSROOM 110
- THE DAILY SCHEDULE 111
- LET'S CHANGE THE SCHEDULE FOR TEACHERS 116
- CHANGE FOR THE SAKE OF CHANGE 116

ACKNOWLEDGMENTS 119

CHAPTER 1

SAFETY IN YOUR CHILD'S SCHOOL

What would you do if your child came home with this story? "I went to the restroom and three guys grabbed me. They took my clothes, pushed my head into a toilet, and squeezed my testicles until I screamed. They left with my clothes and I had to wait until someone came in that would go to the principal for help."

This actually happened, but the local authorities assumed an attitude of "boys will be boys and there isn't much we can do about it." The boy's mother was so upset she shared her frustrations on the Internet. She responded to her son's assault and the indifference of her public school by sending him to a private school.

In another instance, a group of parents determined that their children were afraid to go to school. They went to the school principal and at first the teacher was blamed. After a great deal of time and investigation a different source was found. A pair of young extortion artists was so terrorizing their classmates that the classmates were afraid to tell on them. Those children were in the first grade! Could the same sort of thing happen to your child? It could have already happened and you remain unaware.

The failures of our public schools are swelling the ranks of private schools and of those choosing homeschooling. Many of us don't have the money to send our children to private school, nor do we have the time or inclination for homeschooling. We are forced to pay a great deal of money for our public schools. They have no excuse for our children being fearful of attendance.

YOU AND YOUR CHILD

There is an effort to keep track of school related crime and violence:

http://nces.ed.gov/fastfacts/display.asp?id=49

It is known that crime and violence has affected at least four percent of the student population in 2009-2010. Your child's school may seem safe, but there may be crime and violence that is unknown to you. School officials don't want the news to get out because it makes them look bad and much of the reporting of crime and violence is up them. It takes a hideous crime to make the news. Instances of bullying, drug trade, and theft often go unreported by students because they are fearful or ashamed. It is safe to assume that there is more violence and crime in our schools than is reported—perhaps much more.

You need to take a close look at your school. It may seem that there is little a parent can do, but there are signs of danger and steps you can take to help your child avoid danger. Children may not reveal their fears to parents because parents are apt to storm off to school and make a scene. A frontal attack on teachers and principals is likely to make them defensive and resentful rather than making a difference in the school atmosphere. Children don't want to be embarrassed or pointed out as a squealer because there are apt to be reprisals by school ruffians. Your child is more likely to communicate truthfully if you start out by promising you will not dash off to school and cause a commotion. Assure your child that you can deal with a bad situation in a way that will meet with his or her approval and will not do anything to identify the child as an informant. Then keep your promise!

You must question carefully and thoughtfully about possible fear. A generalized query is apt to result in, "Oh, sure I feel safe." Point out that previous school violence might have been avoided if students had not been reluctant to tell grownups about the impending danger. Reassure your child again that you can handle the situation without making a fuss or pinpointing him or her as the source. (You may be repeating yourself, but it's a proven education technique.) You could ask questions similar to the following.

Are there distractions or interruptions during class? (If so, find out what they are. Chaotic classrooms are signs of unsafe schools.)

Are there ever fights or threats of violence in the halls, the gym, the locker room, the lavatory, or on the playground?

Do you see teachers or principals in these non-classroom areas?

Are there students that threaten other students?

Have you ever been harmed or threatened?

Are there students that pass around pills, powders or small containers they don't want teachers to see?

Have you ever been offered a pill, powder or smoke on the way to or in school?

Do you know of anyone bringing a club, a knife or a gun to school?

Are you sure there is nothing about school that bothers you?

Your child may still be afraid to tell you. Be suspicious if answers are vague or evasive. Immediate use of the bathroom upon returning home may indicate fear of the restroom in school. Wishing to stay home sick when apparently not ill is another clue of unpronounced fear. It could also be a sign they didn't do their homework.

If your child won't tell you, perhaps the teacher will. Ask about school safety in a private situation. Even teachers are open to reprisals from lawless students and from administrators that consider admissions of crime or violence as criticism. Assure the teacher you will keep such information confidential. You might also confide in other parents and ask them to prudently quiz their children. A little detective work on your part could be a salvation for your child.

DEALING WITH THOSE PEOPLE IN SCHOOL

What can you do if you find your child is fearful? In early elementary classrooms a talk with the teacher is in order. To keep your promise to be prudent, a phone call or email might be better than a visit. Depending on the seriousness of the problem, keep in mind that a phone call is much more personal than an email. Request that the teacher keep your call confidential and not bring attention to your child. Explain your child's fear and ask the teacher to discreetly investigate.

If the teacher can't help or betrays your trust, call the school office and ask to speak with the principal. Request for confidentiality and carefully explain the problem. This should get results because the principal is legally the major power in the school. The principal makes the rules and is in charge of students and teachers. Teachers may make classroom rules, but even they are subject to the approval of the principal. Most schools instruct teachers to send serious discipline problems to the principal. Your school should have a written discipline policy that you could read, but what is written and what actually happens could be two different things.

As students progress to middle school they have many teachers, and they find themselves traveling between classes, to the lavatory, the gym, and so on. These "on-your-own" ventures are common sources of trouble. Unless your child's problem is directly tied to one teacher, start right out with a call to the school office.

There is a tendency to look at school discipline in the narrow sense of punishment. We should look at discipline in the broader sense of controlled behavior. It is likely that a disciplined student never needs to be punished. It is possible, but not very probable, that no one in a disciplined school needs to be punished. The best principals can achieve a disciplined school atmosphere with a minimum of punishment. A simple warning from such a principal is usually sufficient because every student knows that failure to heed the warning will lead to swift and uncomfortable punishment.

Despite this power and responsibility, one principal told me he felt his job was to maintain rapport with students, and he could not get too involved with punishments. When a principal dodges the responsibility of discipline and makes teachers the heavy, it commonly results in a disjointed effort that leads to an undisciplined, unsafe school.

In some cases, strong teachers have done a good job with school discipline, but would prefer a strong principal that keeps things running smoothly so they could spend their time teaching instead of disciplining. The following is part of a statement made by a member of my faculty who considered discipline one of our major concerns: *"More has to be done by administrators. They are at the top of the hierarchy and what they do (or don't do) sets the tone for the whole school. If students are rowdy, rude, or disrespectful, then the administrators must set the tone. Teachers need to establish a RAPPORT with students.... This cannot be done while teachers are also expected to play the role of policeman. The roles are mutually exclusive."*

She was totally correct in her appraisal of the role of administrators but rapport and discipline are *not* mutually exclusive;

add the two together and they equal *respect.* The biggest challenge for all educators is to be both a benefactor and authority figure to their students. We cannot have safe schools if principals or teachers neglect either responsibility.

One reason undisciplined, unsafe situations occur is that the obligation of disciplining children is an unpleasant, stressful job, and no one likes the aggravation. Consequently, the lowest man on the administrative totem pole ends up with the duty. Chief administrators sometimes convince school boards that another administrator must be hired to handle discipline so they can do more important things. The highest-paid administrators are often secluded in their offices, staying far away from the crucial problems of discipline, while some poor chump, earning little more than a teacher, is trying to do the toughest, most important task in school. If schools are lucky enough to have principals who are good disciplinarians they tend to move on to become superintendents—sitting behind a desk where their talent is wasted.

There are principals that want to manage a school effectively, but find themselves thwarted on many fronts. Educational and civil law is very restrictive, the system buries them under paperwork and school boards often fail to support their actions. Some time ago Joe Clark made a national name for himself when he tamed an inner-city school with a bullhorn in one hand and a baseball bat in the other. He did not hesitate to remove troublemakers from his school, but he got carried away with his own success. His biggest mistake was suspending dozens of students just because he didn't like their looks. He did prove tough discipline can greatly improve the education atmosphere of a troubled school, but he failed to temper his discipline with justice.

Joe Clark received much acclaim, but he also upset many in the education hierarchy that considered his methods too harsh. Some local parents became hostile, and he was eventually at odds with his school board. Running for a position on the school board is sometimes prompted by a lust for revenge. The harder an administrator works on discipline the more likely he or she is to make enemies. Perhaps that is why so many administrators either evade or downplay this enormous responsibility.

There are administrators that not only accept their responsibilities, they go a step further and eliminate big problems by working on the little ones. For example, the following excerpt is from a letter sent to parents in a local district. It said in part: *"During the short time that I have been here, I have observed some behaviors that both please and concern me. One concern that I have is the number of incidents that begin with students harassing each other. Unfortunately, several of these incidents ended in some sort of student-to-student violence. I spoke on morning announcements today to let the faculty and students know that I am adopting a "zero tolerance" policy in regard to unkind, hurtful, and/or harassing behaviors in the hallway or the classroom. The faculty has been asked to issue one warning and then, if the behavior continues, to send the students to me. I intend to take this negative behavior very seriously. It is my goal that all middle school students should be able to be safe and happy when they are in school. If you have any questions or concerns about this policy or about anything to do with the middle school, I hope that you will feel comfortable in calling or setting up an appointment to see me."*

Some administrators would sit back and rationalize that middle school students picking on one another is natural and must be expected. Who knows how many acts of violence in our schools have stemmed from a few cutting remarks? I called this administrator at 11:00 A.M. to ask for a copy of the letter. I didn't get through because she was in the cafeteria. I finally got in touch with her an hour and a half after the students went home, and she answered the phone herself. She indicated that she saw the need for the letter while walking through the halls. Good disciplinarians don't sit in their office waiting for discipline problems to come to them. They are walking through the school nipping problems in the bud. When I asked her if she got the idea for the letter from graduate school, she laughed and said it was just a matter of common sense. I think I know where she learned diligence and common sense—from the years she spent as a classroom teacher.

Writing the letter was the easy part; enforcing it will take time and effort. It is not a guarantee that future violence will be eliminated, but it represents the kind of effort we should expect from all school principals. She indicated the letter was well received by parents, but it was difficult for some parents to believe their child could be guilty of breaking the rules.

It seems that overprotective, unrealistic parents have done as much to ruin our schools as the parents that don't seem to care. The overprotective ones make statements like, "The school seems more interested in discipline than the needs of my child." They do not seem to realize that self-discipline is the most important lesson learned by any child. The success of a civilized society and its schools depends upon its citizens obeying rules ranging from criminal law to manners. In effect, these parents are telling their child, "Go ahead and disrupt the education of other children if you want; I won't let school authorities pick on you." The most devastating aspect of this frame of mind is that some schools cater to these people and neglect the other students' right to learn in an appropriate atmosphere. We realize that good school discipline is necessary for our children to be safe and to do their best scholastically. We want teachers and principals to have the confidence to stand up to those that believe their child can do no wrong. When you have the opportunity to interact with teachers and administrators let them know you support their efforts toward good discipline.

Even good schools have problems, but bringing them to the attention of the principal should solve them. Continue to check on the situation discreetly. If the principal betrays your trust or can't seem to do anything about the problem—your school is in big trouble, and it is time to go to the superintendent.

If your school system has any size you will probably find the superintendent's office is in a non-school building where he or she is surrounded by a host of non-teachers that aid in the work of running the system. Call the office to arrange a meeting or a phone conversation. You may have to explain what your problem is and what you have done to correct it to one of the helpers, but if you are persistent you may get to talk to the superintendent.

If problems can't be solved, it is because the school board has put an incompetent superintendent in charge of your school system, and your board is not dealing with the situation. The board may not even realize that there are problems. Superintendents like to keep the board sequestered away from outside influences so the board can be more easily controlled. Board members are often told that they shouldn't be dealing directly with parents, teachers, and taxpayers; it is the administrator's right and responsibility to deal with those people. Sadly, board members can become the pawns of the person they have hired to manage their school system.

Complaining at the next school board meeting or going public may have negative results. The superintendent and the board are apt to assume a defensive attitude rather than an understanding one. You may be perceived as "just another troublemaker," and you may be jeopardizing your child. In this situation personal contact with a board member or two is the best way for you to influence how your school is managed. Do not send a letter to the school addressed to the board as a group. An administrator, acting as the representative of the board, will read your letter and may take steps to circumvent your direct contact with board members.

The names of the board members are typically listed in the school newsletter and the school must provide them if asked. If you can't obtain home addresses of board members, a letter sent to the school addressed to a particular board member and marked "personal" should be delivered without being opened.

You may prefer to use the phone, e-mail, or personal contact for communication, but try to keep it short and to the point. Good board members are busy communicating with many people—don't bother them too often nor take up too much of their time or you may end up defeating the whole process.

Ask for mutual confidentiality. Carefully explain the problem, your attempt to solve the problem, and why you are so frustrated that you need to talk to a board member. The board member may be sympathetic, but have no idea what to do about the situation. Explain that insuring your child's school has a competent, hard-working principal with good discipline is the responsibility of the school superintendent. Suggest that the board inform the superintendent that he or she must consider this a primary duty. The evaluation of principals should be on site and comprehensive because things aren't always what they seem. For instance, I know of a situation where the principal was quick to punish regular students, but shied away from hard core troublemakers. The board should follow up by regularly going into executive session (a non-public portion of a regular meeting) without the superintendent to discuss the superintendent's handling of school safety and discipline. A good superintendent should be able to deal with problems quickly and effectively. A host of seemingly insolvable problems is a sign the superintendent is incompetent. Boards must then confront and deal with the superintendent.

In some cases we hear about schools with little or no discipline, but we also hear of discipline gone amuck: a six-year-old was expelled for kissing a classmate; an eleven-year-old was dragged away from school by a deputy sheriff because she put a steak knife in her lunch to cut up her chicken; a seven year old was suspended for apparently chewing a pastry into the shape of a gun. We don't want to see our children unreasonably punished because of such offenses. Our school's primary disciplinarians should be experienced, accomplished educators. If they were allowed to make decisions based on experience rather than a rigid set of rules, we could avoid such ridiculous punishments. The administrators with little experience that "go by the book" have a tendency to cause as many problems as they solve.

Boards can help their schools by actively seeking experienced teachers as administrators. Logically, boards should seek administrators with teaching experience in a situation similar to the one they will administrate. It makes little sense to put a rural elementary person in charge of an inner-city high school or vice versa. It makes no sense to put someone in charge simply because they have a degree from a graduate school.

Another positive board action would be to pay the people that personally handle discipline the highest salaries. That could mean that the vice principal would earn more than the principal. The highest paid person in the superintendent's office would be the person evaluating building disciplinarians. That could mean that the assistant superintendent earns more than the superintendent. This would make those degree-toting position holders howl with indignation. The title "Doctorate" is supposed to get you the most money and excuse you from such unpleasant chores as discipline.

The people of a school district, represented by the board, have the right to pay the most for the most important job.

YOU AND YOUR COMMUNITY

The safety of children falls on the shoulders of three major groups: parents, legal authorities, and the school. There is a tendency for each group to depend on the other two groups to handle the problems. One morning I arrived at school to learn that we had been robbed. My keys and many other sets of keys were missing from the office. The thieves had used them to rob the school of over $10,000 worth of equipment and supplies including my computer and programs. A few days later the perpetrators—some of our own students—were led off in handcuffs. They were apprehended by a teacher who was also a part time police officer. The judge gave them a slap on the wrist, probation, and sentenced them to attend school.

It is unfortunate, but there are youngsters that are so frustrated—or so wicked—that they adopt undisciplined, even criminal behavior. Other children are intelligent, but not wise. They get into trouble because there are no serious consequences. They do not study; after all, they know they will be automatically promoted to the next grade. They see that crime pays and disruptive behavior brings fleeting fame rather than retribution. Consequently, they adopt that behavior. Does sentencing proven criminals to school save the perpetrators or does it make schools into training centers for crime?

When school administrators try to give long suspensions to students that commit serious offenses they are very likely to be opposed by eggheads in the state education department and by civil liberties groups. These people in high places that extol the virtues of keeping each and every teenager in school should be forced to spend a year trying to teach classes that contain teenage criminals. They would find that one or two lawless attendees can devastate a classroom and physically endanger the occupants.

Teenagers are no longer children. Physically and mentally, they can do almost anything adults can accomplish. They also realize our courts and our schools are reluctant to punish youngsters. If young criminals are foolish enough to be apprehended, they suffer few consequences. I have heard several young outlaws brag about their age keeping them from suffering serious punishment. We should stop protecting lawless teenagers and start protecting the students that are their victims.

Public schools have accepted the responsibility of providing the opportunity of education to each and every child. The problem is that this marvelous privilege to obtain a free education has been turned into a self-defeating prerogative. Rather than feeling they have been awarded a wonderful opportunity many children feel condemned to school attendance. If teenagers knew they must study and stay out of trouble to continue in school our public schools would improve dramatically.

Some people erroneously believe forced school attendance will "save" teenagers. This sort of sentiment may sound very caring, but it is just the opposite. It provides an easy escape for the criminal, while disrupting and endangering everyone else in the school. If losing a child means we fail to provide an appropriate education, then we should be ashamed of the large number of children attending our schools that have substandard skills and criminal tendencies. The removal of the very small, truly criminal element would save many borderline students that are now being "lost" because of the detrimental influence of their criminal counterparts.

Private schools, particularly the parochial schools, are often referred to as school systems that get good results while spending half the money per student as public schools. Their ace in the hole is that students are not required to attend. If a child continually misbehaves the privilege to attend the private school is revoked; public schools need the same option. The private schools have also shown they can do a good job with many of the public school's problem children. The reason is that they can show them a no-nonsense, disciplined environment. Most children cease to cause problems when faced with serious consequences.

Should we just turn a thirteen-year-old criminal out into the streets? A year spent on a work farm seems like a better idea. It could be very therapeutic. In the old days we sent youthful lawbreakers to reform school instead of sentencing them to public school. Young, hardened criminals should be the worry of the legal system, not the downfall of the school system.

We can't let our schools and the legal system get away with blaming poor parenting for their failures. On the other hand, some parents resent, resist, or even obstruct the efforts of the other groups. Safe schools require cooperation between all three groups. Your school is a reflection of your community. It is very difficult to have a non-violent, crime-free school when it is located in the middle of a violent, crime-ridden neighborhood. You can make your child's school safer by insisting your school and your legal system provide a safe atmosphere. Let your child know you will support the efforts of the school and the community to provide safe schools even if he or she is disciplined. It is better your child suffer through a little discipline today than becoming part of a disaster tomorrow.

The tragic deaths of 20 students at Sandy Hook Elementary School in Newtown put a knot in our stomachs and questions in our minds. How could anyone be so demented as to kill so many innocent children? Why was it so easy? Who or what is at fault? After the infamous Columbine High School shootings in Littleton,

Colorado a Gallup Poll asked that question. The resulting statistics indicated that the following were tied for the blame.

Media coverage of shocking events

TV, movies, and music

Availability of guns

Parents

Social pressure

The Internet was just behind them. The overall feeling was that government should do something. There should be more regulation of TV, movies, music, and the Internet. Anti-gun people called for more gun control. Others said Social Services should get more money to help parents, and the schools should get more money to help students.

If you are looking to government to make your school safer, you are looking in the wrong direction. You would have to look far and wide to find a public high school that does not have problems with students using drugs and alcohol. Government has responded by surrounding schools in my area with expensive signs declaring "Drug Free School Zone." That's just wishful thinking and a waste of money. It will take much more than putting up signs to make our schools drug free.

It is public knowledge that the federal government can't stop the drug trade. How can it possibly provide you with a safe school? Civilization has always had to deal with crime and violence, and it looks like it always will. Since schools are a part of society, there will always be some crime and deadly violence in our schools. Not a happy thought, but a realistic one. The worst school tragedy happened in Bath Michigan in May of 1927. A bomb exploded under the left wing of the elementary school. When a crowd gathered the perpetrator drove up in his explosive and shrapnel laden car and set it off. Perhaps he was the very first suicide car bomber. He killed 38 children and 6 adults. Unenforceable laws passed by faraway politicians will not make your school safer—they could do just the opposite.

The most perplexing outcome in the Gallup Poll was that the majority of people placed little or no blame on the school. Why are people ready to blame almost anything but the school? It is quite possible that your school is not living up to its responsibility of providing a safe environment. It is very possible it is not prepared to deal with a killer. Ask your school administrator how the school plans to deal with possible deadly violence.

Bear in mind that teachers and school administrators are not trained to deal with crime and violence. Public schools pay teachers extra for accumulating graduate school credits and graduate degrees in education, but teachers might better be paid extra to go to police academy. The kind of training police officers receive would be extremely beneficial to teachers in public schools. Self-control under stress, handling emergencies, protecting themselves and others, recognizing criminal behavior, and the capacity to make an arrest would be much more useful to practicing teachers than a seminar in "Contemporary Issues in Education." If a school's staff included a number of teachers who were also part time law officers, the criminal element would no longer see that school as easy prey.

Teachers that didn't want to be criminologists could pick up some extra pay by developing paramedical skills. If I were a school board member, a teacher candidate that was a part time police officer or paramedic would go to the top of the list. Teachers too meek to be police officers and too queasy to be paramedics would have to live with lower pay and less desirable resumes. There is much more to school than academics. We need a down-to-earth teacher training program that would enable us to staff our schools with people that can physically protect and care for our children.

CHAPTER 2

EFFECTIVE AND DEFECTIVE CLASSROOMS

In the movie *Mary Poppins,* the children wanted a nanny that was never cross or dominating, but rather sweet, kind, witty, and very pretty. The nanny should sing songs, play games, and give treats. Failure to comply with these requirements could result in toads in the bed, hidden spectacles, or pepper in the tea.

Mary Poppins blew in on an east wind that eliminated the competition; she cleaned their rooms with magic; she took them on fantastic trips with a singing, dancing, comedian; then she told them it was stuffy to save money—they might better feed the birds.

Mary Poppins was a well-acted, entertaining fairy tale that I enjoyed along with my children. Of course, it is far from the realities of life. The education elite and parents that expect each teacher to be a real life Mary Poppins are great detriments to excellence in education.

A good example of the "Mary Poppins mindset" was in one of our local papers. A small group of parents complained to the local school board that the first grade class their children were attending was too restrictive. They claimed their children had to sit in their seats and not talk or move all day. Encouraged by the school psychologist, they complained that though puzzles, mazes, and a computer were available in the room, the teacher did not use them during class time. This caused the children to be hyperactive when they got home and resulted in discipline problems for the parents.

The school superintendent pointed out that this particular class was having academic difficulty. Eighty percent were behind in reading when they started the year and he provided the classroom schedule:

8:30 - 9:00 morning program for all students

9:00 - 10:30 class

10:30 - 11:10 lunch

11:10 - 1:15 class

1:15 - 1:30 snack time

1:30 - 2:15 gym or music

2:15 - 2:55 class.

That is a 6½-hour day with 4¼ hours of regular class time broken up into three parts. Does that sound oppressive to you? Those children obviously needed to spend more time on academic activity and less time playing games. The parents should have been commending rather than condemning the teacher for getting their hyperactive children to put in some quality work time. The teacher had the advantage of seventeen years of experience and the parents should have tapped her acquired wisdom. They should have gone to her with thanks and praise—asking for advice on how they could help their children succeed. Instead, they listened to a degree-toting psychologist, complained at a board meeting, and tried to disgrace the teacher publicly. It's a warped society that blames a teacher for working and expecting her students to work.

Those few parents seemed to be more interested in their own problems than they were in the education of their children and were inadvertently robbing other people's children of the opportunity to learn. We seem to live in a time when militant minorities can rule the majority.

Children can learn from playing games, watching educational TV shows, and using computers. However, this kind of learning is haphazard and inefficient. The student must be able to learn specific material in an efficient manner and that requires work. Professional athletes and entertainers have grueling schedules, tough competition, and the pressures of management, the media, the fans, and family. We see some react adversely to all this and mess up their lives despite their golden opportunity. On the other side of the coin, you often hear the most successful professionals say that what they do is fun. What they really mean is they have made the hard work and extra effort fun. There is no way to avoid the work, but the satisfaction of a job well done makes the effort enjoyable.

We that believe children should study while in school have stood idly by and let "fun-theory" educators and small groups of parents change our schools. People who believe in the work ethic will have to stand up and be counted or our public schools will continue to finish way down the list in the Programme for International Student Assessment (Pisa).

http://en.wikipedia.org/wiki/Programme_for_International_Student_Assessment

A CLOSE LOOK AT CLASSROOM ATMOSPHERE

There are many things to consider when it comes to classroom atmosphere. A noisy classroom may represent students working together on a project or toward some other common goal—or it may be that the teacher has lost control. The key is the teacher's ability to attain the attention of the whole group when desired. This must also carry over into times when a student has the floor. Children learn and reinforce their learning by listening to questions and presentations of other students; that is a matter of good sense and good manners.

Teachers have nightmares about dealing with classes that are totally out of control. Maintaining a proper classroom atmosphere is particularly difficult in schools that are poorly managed and have poor discipline policies. One teacher survival technique is to get a student leader on your side—not an academic leader, rather a people leader—a child the other children either respect or fear. Teachers can use special attention, special privilege, special responsibility, or bribery to gain the student's assistance. The student might be a gifted athlete and other students will follow their example. The student might be a bully and the teacher is aiding their thirst for power. Depending on a student to help control the class is a very poor situation, but it is better than complete chaos.

Some teachers resort to class-wide bribery to gain control. They hand out candy, award pizzas, arrange parties, and go on class trips that entertain rather than educate. Bribing students to behave is actually telling them that crime pays, but it is another way to subsist.

Some teachers try to use peer pressure, saying, "So and so was not good today, so the class will not go outside this afternoon and if this behavior continues, the class will not get to go on the field trip." They hope members of the class will convince troublemakers to cooperate. It is a real copout when teachers make the innocent responsible for the guilty, but it is better than no control.

Resorting to unjust and divisive techniques to try to control classes leads to the kind of environment that results in teachers and students being branded as underachievers. If teachers are lucky enough to work in a school system with a responsible administration and a good discipline process, they will not have to resort to such subterfuges. All they have to do is let the students know they are aware of the school rules and intend to see that they are followed.

This is the kind of environment that produces good students and accomplished teachers.

In poor circumstances some teachers take the bull by the horns and get tough. Your child is apt to come home and saying the teacher was mean to me. For example, the following were not calm words of advice uttered in a private conference. I was giving Bob the business in front of the whole geometry class: *Bob, what in the heck is wrong with you? You're fooling around in class, you're not getting your homework done and you messed up the last test. Do you think you're somebody special and don't have to do any work around here? If you don't shape up, you're headed for a rude surprise when report cards come out.*

What if Bob was your child and he came home grumbling that he had been harassed and embarrassed? Some parents would immediately complain to everyone from the principal to the president of the school board. It is more appropriate for you to take into account the fact you are getting a one-sided view of the situation. If you felt Bob had been wronged, a call to the teacher is in order to get their side of the story. Then you have to decide whether to call the school's principal or tell Bob he had better start working in geometry.

There is a theory that teachers being sweet and kind will result in students being that way. Teachers prefer to use this tact, but it doesn't always work. There are students who look on this as a sign of weakness and try to usurp authority. It is the duty of responsible teachers to maintain control even if they have to resort to being unpleasant.

When Lou Holtz left as coach of Notre Dame's famous football team; he was surprised that his players were sorry to see him go. While being interviewed on ESPN, he said in essence that he always thought that if he were murdered the investigation would be hopeless—there would be too many suspects. For some reason, few people object to coaches demanding attention, publicly pointing out failures, and insisting on extra personal effort. The classroom teacher at any level of education that operates in this fashion may be in for a tough time. Perhaps it is because the results of poor discipline are so much more obvious on the athletic field than in the classroom. If teachers insist students behave and work, they are mean, cruel, and not interested in their students' welfare. On the other hand, if teachers fail to make students behave and they are injured the teacher may be accused of negligence. If the students won't work the teacher may be blamed for their failure. There are no universal solutions to such catch-22 situations.

My scolding of Bob made an "I'll show him" look appear in his eyes. We didn't have very many sociable words during the rest of the year, but he did get back to work. We were not really friends again until the last day of school when I shook his hand to congratulate him for earning 100% on the state geometry test. He went on to be one of my best students and now uses his math to earn a living. They say you can kill people with kindness—a few harsh words can be a lifesaver.

Then there was the girl in my general math class that had some problems. One day she got up and left the room just as class was about to start. I followed her down the hall into study hall. Herb was in charge, and I told him she was from my class and we might as well leave her there. Later in the faculty room, Herb commented that it was not like me to let a student get away with such behavior. I told him that in this particular case making a fuss would probably do more harm than good. She was back the next day and there were no more major problems.

In these two instances, I apparently made the correct decisions. I prefer not to tell you about the times I made mistakes.

Of course I have some excuses. My college training was totally academic and had nothing to do with the harsh realities of public school discipline. The administrators of my schools were frequently weak or indecisive disciplinarians. Schools are a far cry from the fairy tale world of Mary Poppins and the "heads in the clouds" theories of academia. I had to try my best under poor circumstances, but I am sure that as I gained experience I was more likely to make the right disciplining choice.

What do you do when the school sends you a discipline report concerning classroom behavior? Before you do anything, put yourself in the shoes of teachers and principals. Teachers must set reasonable rules for their classroom and explain what will happen if the rules are broken. Most importantly, when tested—and they are often tested—they must do what they promised. If the teacher writes a detailed report of disruptive behavior the principal should have little choice but to take action. Then the teacher and the principal can lean back and wonder if they will have to deal with an irate parent rather than an open minded, concerned parent. I hope this gives you a more sympathetic view of your school's efforts to maintain a disciplined classroom atmosphere.

We all know how difficult it is to deal with children properly. Parents, teachers, and administrators should be working together to resolve classroom problems. All too often, the teacher wants the child punished; the parents think the child was wronged; and the administrator seeks the easy way out rather than justice. It is a disservice to the child when all three are pulling in different directions. Collaboration between all parties involved cannot be legislated or learned in college. Good school discipline may upset your child occasionally, but it is protecting him or her from far greater evils and providing the opportunity to learn. You can't expect the process to be perfect. When mistakes or inequities occur, parents and school personnel must work with one another to resolve them. We can't let minor flaws destroy the process.

Teachers can be tough if they are fair, and once real control is achieved, teachers can let students know they are human and interested in other things than just hitting the books. The line between too tough and too lenient is hard to distinguish—it depends on the teacher and the members of the class. Experience is what helps accomplished teachers know when to be firm and when to be lenient.

CHARACTERISTICS OF GOOD CLASSROOM TEACHING

A well disciplined class is necessary, but not sufficient for good education. There are other considerations.

Do your child's classes prepare him or her to do homework? Assigned work is the student's opportunity to do the task and it is the most important aspect of learning. A long lecture that goes over the heads of the class and sends them home unprepared to do their homework is a total waste of precious time. You should be concerned if your child comes home from school and doesn't know how to do homework assignments. It could be the teacher's fault; it could be your child's fault; or it could be a little of both. Teachers should not be rated on the amount of work they do; they should be rated on their ability to prepare their students to work.

If the problem persists, it is time to contact the teacher. Carefully explain the problem and ask for suggestions. For example, "Jane doesn't seem to have any idea of how to do her homework and it is difficult for me to help her. I wondered if you might have some suggestions that would help us?" This should create a positive relationship between you and the teacher. The teacher may provide you with some helpful suggestions. Realizing this is a problem might cause the teacher to make some positive changes and you have improved your child's classroom. You might find out that Jane just doesn't pay attention. That is a tough problem to solve, but you and the teacher working together are in the best position to obtain positive results. If your school is properly managed and staffed with well-trained teachers, there will be a minimum of difficulties and an excellent chance of proper solutions. Sadly, our current system often fails to provide us with that kind of school.

Does your child know if she or he did their homework correctly? Homework is practice that will lead to success in tests because practice presents the opportunity to correct errors. Math teachers may provide answers to the homework the next day and solve missed problems in class. Teachers that assign essays must face the grueling task of correcting each one, pointing out errors and making suggestions. This is wasted work if students do nothing more than look at the grade. You can help your child by being just as concerned about the correction of yesterday's homework as you are about the completion of tomorrow's homework. If it appears your child is not correcting homework and learning from his or her mistakes, a call to the teacher may help. In a poor situation, you may have to take the responsibility of constantly monitoring your child's correction of homework.

Does your child get immediate feedback after taking a test? There is much more to a test than a grade because students learn by correcting their recent mistakes. Even students receiving a 100% grade benefit from going over the material one more time, for it helps them prepare for the final exam. Parents should ask to see their child's test papers as soon as they are returned. Math tests should be returned the next day. Tests that require a great deal of writing could take longer. Find out if the teacher went over the test in class or marked it in such a way that it becomes a teaching tool as well as an evaluating device. If you find tests are not properly used, it is time to talk to the teacher.

Does your child's teacher provide personal help? Teachers usually provide help if asked, but a high school teacher with more than a hundred students doesn't have the time to help every student every day. Ask your child if he or she has the opportunity to ask for help when needed. Then ask if he or she takes advantage of the opportunity. Many students (for various reasons) are reluctant to ask for help. Perhaps your child needs help, but is too bashful to ask. If you can't convince them to ask for help, a discreet call to the teacher might solve the problem. Explain the situation and ask if the teacher can find a way to provide a little help without embarrassing your child. Most teachers are sympathetic and willing to take extra steps if the circumstances are explained to them.

Perhaps your child can find a classmate who will help. I encouraged my best students to help others while students were working on their homework in class. Of course they weren't allowed to copy each other. One student might ask another, "What did you get for number nine?" If they didn't agree, they would have to figure out who made the mistake and what it was. Helping others made my best students even better and some went on to become teachers.

Does your child know what to expect when she or he goes to class? Many highly placed educators would say that sticking to a routine does not show enough teacher innovation. Administrators (many of whom know only what they learned in college) compound this problem by favoring the "innovative" teachers over those that are diligent. In reality, some students need structure and are confused by classes that do not follow regular patterns. Something different once in a while is acceptable, but teachers that constantly strive to amaze and amuse students can be detracting from their student's education. If your child continues to be in the dark about what will happen tomorrow, it warrants some interaction with your child's teacher. For example, if your child has a bit of autism explain that he or she needs structure and knowing what will happen in class ahead of time would be a great help. Your call could lead to positive changes.

Do some teachers in your child's school resort to bribery as a teaching technique? It is unfair and divisive. Should financially flush teachers be allowed to usurp student time and interest from teachers with many financial obligations such as their family and their mortgage? Your child may think the teacher that gives the best bribes is the best teacher, but you are wise enough to know that is not necessarily true. Our schools should strive to make the youth of our nation understand education is its own reward—classroom bribes send the opposite message. Talk to those people in school; tell them the decision to bribe or not to bribe should be yours—not the teacher's.

Does your high school teach your child how to study? The ability of students to study on their own is considerably more important than any number of facts a teacher can cram into their heads. When our children go off to college, their most damaging deficiency is ignorance of study methods. I believe there is a tendency for high school teachers to assume that all students have developed good study methods. Ask your child's high school teachers if they are teaching study methods appropriate for college. The answer may not be very satisfying because it's not part of the curriculum. However, just asking the question will draw the teacher's attention to something that he or she may be neglecting.

Since the students' test scores are now used to judge teachers, there is a great deal of pressure to get sub-par students through their classes. Consequently, the teachers end up doing all the work for them. Students are released from study responsibilities at the very time in their lives they should be learning them. With their teachers doing everything for them, they don't learn how to take good notes and use them, they can't outline a chapter and they don't know how to study for a test. There are better ways to evaluate teachers. When we know we have good teachers in place, we can put more of the responsibility of learning on our children. In the long run they will be better prepared to deal with the realities of life.

REVISITING THE EDUCATION CHAIN OF COMMAND

Knowledgeable parents asking knowledgeable questions can significantly improve their child's classroom experience. Don't be afraid to do your part! When you perceive a classroom problem, contact the teacher. You and the teacher working as allies are in the best position to solve the problem quietly. Going directly to the top may alienate the teacher, muddy the waters, embarrass your child, or cause other repercussions.

The best method of contact is a discreet phone call. Emails are acceptable if the problem is not very serious. Teachers of art, music, gym, as well as middle school teachers and high school teachers deal with many students each day. Don't become upset if your child's name does not immediately ring a bell. Be prepared to tell the teacher when your child is scheduled with him or her and a description might also help. Bear in mind you only know what your child has told you and you want to form your own conclusions.

If contact with the teacher is unproductive the parent should go to the school principal, who is responsible for the evaluation of teachers. If the parent does not like the principal's actions, the next step is to contact the district superintendent. If all else fails, contact with board members is in order.

It may take administrators and/or board members a long time to solve problems so the parent can consider other actions such as a different school, or a media-attracting trip to a school board meeting. Parents should do some careful investigation and some serious soul searching before taking drastic actions or creating a big public fuss. For every action there is a reaction, and needless bad publicity is not good for the school, the teacher, the parent, and especially the child. However, there are times and situations where a big public fuss is required to make needed changes.

Parenting is an awesome task. On a personal scale, it is a position of extreme influence and power. As our children get bigger, so do the problems. It's tough when children think you are just being mean. Eventually they may appreciate your efforts, but it's easier to let them do what they want instead of insisting they do what they should. We must make tough decisions as to when to be authoritarian and when to be supportive. Sometimes we interfere too much; sometimes we do too little. We parents can do no more than try our hardest and hope for the best. We must realize growing children all too quickly take charge of their own destinies. There is an old platitude that I changed into what I call

The Parent's Prayer:

God grant me

The serenity to accept the things I cannot change,

The courage to change the things I should change,

The patience to accept things I dislike, but should not change,

And the wisdom to know the difference.

CHAPTER 3

TESTS: HOW THEY SHOULD BE USED AND HOW TO IMPROVE SCORES

While in elementary school my son received an A in reading. I was quite pleased until I carefully studied the whole report card. Tucked away down at the bottom of the other page was a little graph indicating he was an entire year below his grade level. That bit of information came from a standardized test. I asked his teacher how he could be so far behind and still get an A. It was because "he tried hard." What do the grades students receive on their report cards really mean? If Johnny can't read and no one knows it—including Johnny—it is no surprise he doesn't learn.

ABOUT STANDARDIZED TESTS

Standardized tests differ from classroom tests because they compare your child's test results to the results a very large group of children in the same grade that took the same test or a similar test. Such tests are produced commercially, by states, and by the federal government. The results can be reported as percentiles scores that range from 0 as a low to 100 as a high. A score of 50 is in the middle, meaning that there are just as many students that got higher scores as got lower scores. The education elite may take it upon themselves to pick percentile ranges to be reported to schools in such terms as grade level or perhaps as unacceptable, acceptable, good, or excellent.

The No Child Left Behind Act (NCLB) demands that all fourth and eighth graders be tested with the National Assessment of Educational Progress (NAEP) standardized test every two years to check on state standardized testing. The NCLB requires states to intervene when local schools have too many low standardized test scores. This rejects the notion that a school could be doing a good job, but have a large population of struggling students. If the state takeover is not successful, the school can be closed. The NCLB also makes provisions for parents to remove their children from such schools and send them elsewhere.

The NCLB has turned out to be cumbersome and ineffective. A typical result when federal government interferes with daily living. The federal government has recently revised the NCLB. Chances are it will be just as cumbersome and just as ineffective. Standardized tests continue to be used by government to evaluate schools and their teachers. That jumps right over the proper use of standardized testing. These test scores should be used to help local educators evaluate individual students.

When standardized tests show certain students are not achieving minimum skills, the obvious action is failure. However, some "educators" theorize that failing a student is traumatic and does not result in academic improvement. In my experience it is the other way around. We made a mistake with our son and either sent him to school too early or failed to prepare him properly. He didn't do well and eventually the school tried a special program that wasn't working. Consequently, we decided to hold him back a year. *We didn't fail the school—we failed the child.* Our failure had resulted in his failure. It was not easy on him or us. However, he became an honor student, graduated from college, and works for a high tech company. It benefits students, parents, and schools to honestly face the facts rather than trying to make everyone "feel good." The "no-one-fails" policy encourages students to remain lethargic. Real life is full of failures and the most successful people can relate back to failures because those failures spurred them on to success.

I'm not a good singer so I don't sing around others. When I was a boy I didn't knew the difference; someone had to take the responsibility of telling me. That honest appraisal has saved me from embarrassment and many others from audio discomfort. None of us are exactly alike. We all have our strengths and our weaknesses. Classroom strategies that try to make every child the same are a disservice to the individual and the society.

Our local Director of Curriculum and Instruction informed me that a large book company produced the tests given in my school district, but New York State would probably begin producing its own tests. The tests are called "secure" and no one but the makers may see them. Parents and teachers have no idea what is on the tests or how they are scored. When a school tells you they are giving a "secure" test it really means that the tests are secure from outside scrutiny and criticism.

Although our school gives secure tests, the maker does supply a sample test. Hoping the sample test was a reliable representation of the actual test; I looked it over. The Grade 4 Mathematics Test was given in two books. The first book contained thirty multiple-choice questions. The first two questions were standard arithmetic problems with no words (multiplication and subtraction). The remainder of the test consisted of word problems requiring the student to identify the problem, develop a solution method and obtain the correct answer.

The second book contained eighteen questions, each with two parts, for a total of thirty-six questions. Students had to write the answers and were often required to show work or make explanations. The entire test included seventeen multi-step questions. There were nine number theory questions (questions about the structure of our number system, rather than its use), six geometric shape problems (including the trapezoid and parallelogram), four probability questions, four inequality questions, and three metric system questions. The math section of this fourth grade test was clearly a reading test about mathematics. The test seemed much more concerned with pointing out the mathematically brilliant than determining the abilities of nine-year-olds to use the arithmetic of everyday living.

Although the test makers often claim that it does not help to prepare students for such tests, everyone in education knows that it does. Teachers respond by preparing students to take the tests instead of preparing them for life. I remember a fellow math teacher telling me he could learn how to do math problems, but he often failed to understand the finer points of mathematical theory. He said he was a doer rather than a thinker. Tests aimed toward the doers seem to fit more nicely into the intent of the No Child Left Behind Act, but the test I reviewed seems to be bypassing those that are doers. Should elementary students spend their time studying higher math topics while failing to learn arithmetic?

The first section of the language arts test consisted of answering questions about five different reading presentations, which included a poem. In the second section, students were to read a selection two times and could take notes. Afterward, students could use their notes to answers several questions. There was also a writing-about-a-topic question. Finally, there was a read two selections and answer questions about them section. One of those questions required a written response. The language arts section of the test also seemed to be on the tough side for fourth graders, but to be fair, this is not my field.

HOW YOU CAN USE YOUR CHILD'S STANDARDIZED TEST SCORES

If the school does not provide you with your child's standardized test results—ask for them. Compare your child's standardized test scores to their grades. A child with high scores, but with Bs or less on report cards is either not working up to potential in class or is improperly taught. On the other hand, a child with low standardized scores, but receiving passing grades needs help. The school should point out these kinds of discrepancies. If they don't, be sure you point them out to the school. It is sad that the federal government has forced schools into being more interested in obtaining a high percentage of students reaching a minimum standard than using standardized tests to deal with the needs of individual students. It is a step toward mediocrity rather than excellence.

CLASSROOM GRADING

Though classroom grading is one of the most important duties of teachers, it is one of the most neglected. Colleges provide would-be teachers with a course in the theory of statistics that has little or no practical application to the grading of students. Most schools do little more than tell teachers what kind of grading they can use.

A letter grading system with eight grades (F, D, C, C+, B, B+, A, A+) is adequate for grading. There are too many variables to give more grades, especially grades to the nearest percent. If you told teachers they had to choose from forty different descriptive grades, they would say it was ridiculous, but some will tell you they can tell the difference between an 84% and an 85% student.

A common misconception is that a report card grade of 85% indicates that a student has learned 85% of the material every student should learn about that subject. In reality what should be learned varies from state to state, school to school, and even classroom to classroom. Although 85% may appear to be a precise grade, it is nothing more than a teacher's estimate of how well a student is doing in his or her class.

Another fallacy is that "average students" will receive C grades. When one looks at the spread of marks, it is obvious that a grade of C does not represent average achievement. Rather, it warns that the student is at one of the lower levels. I can tell you from experience that hard-working, students of average intelligence can obtain As and Bs, while the very intelligent, but less than diligent students, can slip to lower levels. A report card full of Cs and Ds is a sign something is wrong. The child may need remedial help, a change in program, or an attitude adjustment.

The normal curve, touted by statistics class, indicates that the bulk of student scores should be near the middle of the scale. That should *not* apply to your child's classroom! If students are properly prepared and placed in appropriate courses, most of the marks will be B or above. If failing students and low achievers are passed, many of the marks should be below B.

Students don't end up in appropriate courses because the current trend is to treat everyone as academic equals. Designating courses as college entrance, intermediate, or remedial is called "Tracking" and is a current no-no in education. Heaven forbid we label students because it will damage their psyche and doom them to sub-performance. I know this is false because I taught a remedial math course that students took in addition to their regular math class. It did not doom them to a life of inferior academic achievement. In some cases, the extra work and guidance helped those children become successful students. Pointing out students' deficiencies and making an effort to deal with them is a true act of compassion; ignoring deficiencies is dereliction of duty.

One of the more difficult grading decisions a teacher makes is giving a grade to a student that is on the borderline between grades. This is the subjective part of the already arbitrary process of grading. Extra work and participation can be considered when performance falls between two grades. Suppose a student receives percent scores of 94, 92, 75, 95, 93. That would be just below 90 and a B+ on the report card. However, any child can have a bad test day because of illness or personal problems. If I thought the student just had a bad day and was really an A student, I would put A on the report card. Neither would I drastically lower a student's grade just because the student was a discipline problem. The threat of low marks to deal with bad attitudes is a bad attitude. Teachers should be judging their students' academic achievements separately from their personalities. If your school is properly administered, this questionable grading technique will not be found because discipline problems will be handled by other means.

Classroom marks that are totally based on class participation or projects are nebulous and should be considered as bonus grades. This can be a teacher's way of transferring the burden of conducting class to the students. The teacher doesn't have to teach or devise and correct tests. All this teacher has to do is show up to class and pull a mark out of the air. A course in high school that uses these techniques exclusively should not receive a grade, but a simple pass or fail. However, these techniques should not be excluded because some college courses are conducted in this manner.

Students should not be penalized for errors in homework—neither should they receive high grades on something so easily copied. Chronic failure to do homework will automatically reduce the grade and should be considered a discipline problem.

Quizzes should not be a major factor in grading because they reflect understanding rather than learning. A student may understand how to do something today, but if they cannot perform a similar task tomorrow, in two weeks, or two months, they have not learned the concept.

Some teachers are known as easy markers and are probably trying to win favor and friendship by making everyone feel good. Other teachers are just the opposite. They give low marks unless the student does something exceptionally brilliant. Most teachers find themselves somewhere between these two extremes. Sometimes students receive unrealistically high grades that interfere with good education, while other times they receive undeserved low grades that are a discouragement. Students and parents deserve an honest estimation of accomplishment—something they are not always obtaining from our schools.

Every school should have a clearly defined grading system that can easily be explained to parents. Teachers should not necessarily obtain their marks in the same manner, but there should be some consistency concerning such things as the meaning of a C grade. Parents, students, teachers, and other school staff should all be viewing the grades in the same light.

Look into the grading policies of your school. They might be available in the school newsletter or your child's student handbook. If they are not—call the school and ask for them. If the policy is not clear, do not be afraid to ask questions. Go to open house and ask teachers and the principal what a mark of C means. You may be surprised at the variety of answers. Questions from parents like yourself may force your school to take the grading of students more seriously.

THE TEACHER AND CLASSROOM TESTS

When grading is based primarily on test scores, devising a test is a big responsibility. Choosing test questions is a complex task. Teachers want to cover all the material, but the test cannot be too long, too easy or too difficult. Teachers should preview their test, which means doing the test before they give it to the students. If they find the test is too short, too long, too tough, or too easy they must make changes. One sad fact teachers have to keep in mind is that students are often poor readers and the more verbiage in the questions, the lower the scores. Devising a good test involves many tough decisions, but experience helps. You have little control over this aspect of education. However, you can ask your child's teacher how he or she develops a test. Your interest and comments may have a positive influence upon the teacher.

How do teachers react if they give a test and most of the marks are very low? First, there must be some soul searching. Did the students fail to prepare, or did the teacher unsatisfactorily present the material? Was the test too hard? Even with experience, it is possible to come up with a test that is simply too difficult.

One way to handle a testing bomb is to quickly review the material and give a retest. Individuals that may have done well on the first test should not be penalized; so if a retest was needed I would simply record both tests. Teachers cannot give a retest very often or students would come to expect two tests and the teacher would end up using too much time testing.

Sometimes, when test marks are obviously too low, high school teachers curve grades by giving higher marks than actually obtained on the test. On the other end of the scale, elementary teachers that are instructing students in the basics should not curve grades. Everyone should learn the basics and a proper evaluation is necessary. There is a tendency for the vast differences between elementary and high school education to be misunderstood or ignored.

There are purists totally against curving grades, but it is commonly done. The college entrance tests are a good example. Answering only half the questions correctly on the SAT college entrance test might result in an above average test score. As students become older, they should realize they must never give up on a test even when the test seems impossible.

Some educators claim there is too much testing in schools. However, the state requires you take a test to drive a car, as well as become a beautician, certified electrician, accountant, teacher, airplane pilot, boat captain, doctor, lawyer, or hold a civil service job. The list is endless. There is also a long federal government list, which includes such large groups as the armed services and the post office. When you stop and think about it, the most important skill students acquire in school is the ability to do well on a test; it is a skill that everyone should hone to the best of their ability.

STUDENT PREPARATION FOR TESTS

It is common to hear students say they understand, but they just can't do well on tests. A reading deficiency is a common cause of poor test scores. Many tests, including math tests, become just as much a test of reading as a test of the subject matter. This is a major reason elementary grades need to place a great deal of emphasis on reading. If your child is not reading well, there are ways for parents to help overcome reading deficiencies (Chapter 4).

Students must learn how to prepare for a test and develop good test taking techniques. A child in middle or high school that reads well and still has problems with tests probably doesn't know how to prepare for a test or just doesn't bother. You can help your child by asking when tests will be given and monitoring his or her efforts to prepare for the test.

First of all they must have the information to be tested at their disposal. To help my students (7-12) attain this goal I recommended they keep a loose-leaf notebook. That allowed them to keep their homework, classroom notes, study sheets, and tests in appropriate order. A notebook is the successful student's most valuable tool. It contains the material the teacher emphasized, along with homework questions and their answers, all of which are typically on the test. Diligently doing homework and keeping a notebook can greatly reduce test preparation time. You could help your child by providing materials for notebooks and looking them over once and a while.

If the child fails to keep a good notebook, the textbook should provide most of the essential information. Classes that use handouts and try to operate without textbooks can put some students at a disadvantage. It is tough enough for them to keep track of a textbook. Keeping track of a year's supply of loose paper can be too much. There is nothing more discouraging than sitting down to study for a test with a disheveled pile of papers knowing that many important ones are missing. The value of a loose leaf notebook and paper punch greatly increases in this type of class.

The next step is to list the topics to be covered and to determine the important facts and/or procedures that must be learned for each topic. The easiest way to accomplish this is to look through a good notebook. Teachers do not keep the topics that are going to be on the test a secret. In most cases I reviewed the all the material to be tested the day before the test. Of course, the test questions were *not* part of the review. A good set of notes from this in-class review would be of great value, but students must first develop a note-taking habit. The alternative to a good notebook is to outline the given section of the textbook or sort through a pile of papers.

As my students matured, my methods changed. It was my experience in college that the professors did not review for tests and were apt to have moved on to new material before the test on the old material was given. Consequently, by the time my students were seniors I did not provide a pretest review. They had to go through their notebooks, pick out the key material, and perhaps ask me questions. Some people may have thought my failure to provide review was negligence, but when students enter college they must have acquired the ability to prepare for a test on their own.

The toughest and most neglected step is memorizing the essential material. It certainly isn't fashionable to make a concentrated effort to learn essential information, but it's the key to good grades. Just looking through the notes or reading the chapter won't do for most students. One way to memorize is to write. When students can spell a word or write a formula without looking at it, they are well on their way to having it memorized. To be sure, they should write it several more times, and try again later or the next morning. Having someone quiz the student on the required material is also a big help. This is a great way for students to help each other and for parents to help their child.

TEST DAY STRATEGIES

There are specific test-taking techniques and attitudes that students can use to achieve their best scores.

Get a good night's sleep and eat breakfast.

Listen closely to all direction given by the teacher.

Ask questions if you are unsure of what to do.

Don't worry about being nervous—nervousness helps! Your body is preparing to meet the challenge, and you are sharper than usual.

Read directions and questions carefully, paying close attention to punctuation and qualifying words such as NOT, EXCEPT, MOST, LEAST, and GREATEST.

Work steadily, but not hastily. If you find you have difficulty finishing tests in the allotted time or that you are one of the last ones done, you should work on increasing speed. Quickness is an asset in sports and in test taking. Sometimes students don't realize this and don't even try to work steadily. On the other hand, if you find you are one of the first ones done, but make silly mistakes, you should slow down and pay more attention to details.

If you don't know how to answer a question, you should temporarily skip it and finish the test. Be sure to also skip the question on your answer sheet! You can't afford to let tough questions upset you or prevent you from finishing the test. After you get through the remainder of the test, you can go back and tackle the tough problems. Sometimes the time spent away from the problem provides the insight needed for its solution.

If you go back to a math question, the best way to check it is to do it again without looking at your previous work. Following your own work tends to lead to the same mistakes.

Panic is an enemy that freezes the mind or body into inaction. If you suddenly feel you "just can't think" you can try the following:

(1) Take a deep breath and yawn; it may seem silly but it helps you relax.

(2) Close your eyes and think of something pleasant for a few seconds.

(3) Do something—a good try may gain credits, a blank will not.

(4) *Be prepared!* A well-prepared test taker is too busy working to let panic destroy concentration.

COLLEGE ENTRANCE TESTS

The largest and toughest standardized tests students face are the college entrance tests. The first one is the Preliminary Scholastic Aptitude Test/National Merit Scholarship Qualifying Test (PSAT/NMSQT). Students take the test during their junior year. As the name implies, it is an introduction to SAT testing. Students find out what the test is like and see how well they score. The results are not used for college entrance, but the National Merit Scholarship program uses them. How can it be merely practice if the scores count toward scholarships? The better students, who feel they have a chance for a scholarship, should prepare as diligently for the PSAT as they would for the SAT.

The SAT is not the only college entrance test; there is also the American College Test (ACT). The ACT is an achievement oriented test that asks straightforward questions similar to those asked in school. The old SAT was a reasoning test that leaned much more toward intelligence testing than achievement. The current SAT is longer and slanted a bit more toward achievement. Diligent, hard working students would probably do better on the ACT while students with high IQs would probably do better on the SAT.

The tests are given at various times throughout the year and students must pay to take them. It is part of your school guidance counselors' duties to help students make proper arrangements. Commonly, students take the entrance tests at the end of their junior year so they can have the results sent to colleges of their choice during their senior year. This also provides the opportunity for a second try if the first score is lower than expected. Second tries take time, effort, and more money, so it is better to be properly prepared in the first place.

Most colleges will accept the SAT or the ACT, but you should check out the colleges you plan to send an application. School guidance counselors or the reference section of libraries will have books that provide information on entrance requirements for every college. These books also give you an idea of how difficult it may be to be accepted at the more prestigious colleges.

There is some controversy about student's preparation for these tests. The test makers say special study for the test is not necessary, but entrepreneurs are making money selling study material and providing guided study sessions. The test makers provide preparation in the booklets "Taking the ACT Assessment," "Taking the PSAT," "Taking the SAT," and "Taking the SAT II: Subject Tests." Your school's guidance counselor(s) should distribute them well before the tests, but you may have to ask for them.

These booklets contain information about the test questions, as well as a sample test. It is important that students thoroughly study these booklets and familiarize themselves with the tests. Professional golfers acquaint themselves with a golf course before the tournament starts because knowing the layout of the course is a definite advantage. The same applies to test taking. For instance the SAT penalizes wrong answers so blind guessing is not a good idea. The ACT does not penalize wrong answers so answering every question is a good idea.

The ACT and SAT have online preparation and sell used tests at a price considerably lower than the cost of commercial preparation courses. If several tests are scored, reviewed, and incorrect responses analyzed, the student is apt to see a substantial increase in their score. After two or three practice tests the student will also have a good idea of what their score should be on the real test. Theoretically, students should be able to handle this kind of preparation on their own, but in actual practice even the best students may never get around to doing one practice test. Some students spend the time and money to take both tests and submit the best result to the college. Trying sample tests under test conditions would be a cheaper way to make this assessment.

Sometimes English and math teachers are asked to use a regular class period to help students prepare for the tests. It would take twenty class periods to do a good job, and teachers can't rob students of that much class time. An ineffectual stab at test preparation may make parents and the school administrator feel better, but does little to help students. Your high school should provide at least twenty hours of guided instruction in college entrance test preparation by qualified teachers outside of regular school hours. Teachers would help students study the test booklets and become familiar with directions, different types of questions, and appropriate test taking techniques. Students should then have the opportunity to take sample tests under test conditions. Teachers should help students correct the tests and provide solutions as well as answers. It is particularly important to know what the examiners will be looking for in the SAT essay. Teachers should then help students convert the raw scores into standard test scores. Understanding the curved marking systems will give students more confidence and higher scores.

Why is it that school superintendents would rather spend money on fancy new programs or machines than pay teachers extra for outside the classroom work in college entrance test preparation? They are missing a golden opportunity to raise test scores and help students learn some of the material they missed along the way.

Outside of hiring private help, you and your child will probably have to do the preparation on your own.

Colleges use the test scores, along with class average, special attributes, achievements, recommendations, and the student's application, as the criteria for student selection. Most colleges will tell you the test score is a minor aspect of the selection process. Some colleges, submitting to the age of mediocrity, do not require them. The reality is that the prestigious colleges, with many more applications than they can accept, are much more likely to admit a student that can provide a high score on a college entrance test. The less renowned colleges accept lower scores and then on down the line until you reach the colleges that will accept almost anyone that can put the money together. It may not be fair, but the prestige level of the college you attend can greatly influence your future.

Some colleges require or recommend prospective students take SAT II: Subject Tests. These one-hour tests measure knowledge and the ability to use that knowledge. Over twenty tests fall under five headings: English, History and Social Studies, Mathematics, Sciences, and Languages. Colleges may use the results as part of the selection process or to place students in proper courses.

The Educational Testing Service produces the PSAT, SAT I, and the SAT II for the College Board. Paying for all those tests and proper preparation gives parents a taste of what it's like to have a child in college. Although the College Board is a not-for-profit organization, it provides some wonderful jobs for college types. Parents should realize that those learned college types are just as interested in getting your dollar as educating your child. The way college costs keep going up; one wonders if colleges have replaced intellectual integrity with monetary greed.

There are people that recommend that college entrance tests be eliminated. They point out that test scores are nothing more than a rough estimate of student achievement and skills. They feel there are more important elements of intellectual development, such as critical thinking and social interaction. These people choose to ignore that students need acceptable skills in reading, writing, and arithmetic to reach their full potential as great thinkers. Testing is the only way colleges have to be sure students have developed those essential skills.

Suppose you were a parachutist learning to pack your own chute. Would you want the instructor to demonstrate chute packing and then walk away without checking your ability to pack the chute? Evaluation through testing provides essential information for proper educational development. Without this information plans for the future are just a shot in the dark. Our testing techniques may not be perfect (what is?), but they represent the best system we have.

CHAPTER 4

LEARNING THE NEGLECTED BASICS

THE DEMEANING OF ARITHMETIC

The Mathematical Sciences Education Board National Research Council says elementary (grades K-4) "Must include substantial subject matter other than arithmetic, including basic elements of geometry, measurement, data analysis, and probability." Basic probability involves ratios, fractions, and percent. Some far off eggheads want children that trying to master basic arithmetic to study probability. These people don't seem to realize that once a student knows the basic operations of arithmetic he or she can be taught probability with a minimum of effort. On the other hand, the study of probability is always hampered by poor arithmetic skills. The introduction of probability at this level is not necessarily the evil; the evil is that such studies are replacing the age old practice of learning arithmetic.

The decline of arithmetic skills can be traced to the introduction of the number line to teach addition. To make a basic number line, you mark off equal spaces on a line and label them with consecutive whole numbers. If you want to add three to five, you start at five and count three more spaces to land on the answer. The theory behind this technique is that students can see how addition works and thus better understand the concept. The reality is that students learn to add by counting and they continue to add by counting for the rest of their lives.

As youngsters, we learned our sums and could provide the result almost instantaneously. That is no longer the case. When I was still teaching, I would give each new group of seventh graders a verbal addition quiz with lots of time between questions. Almost everyone would answer all the questions correctly. Then I would give the same test, allowing just enough time between questions to write down the answer. Rarely did anyone correctly answer all the questions because they relied on the counting method. There were twelfth grade students in my college entrance class adding eight and five by starting at eight and counting five things—sometimes on their fingers, sometimes using marks on their paper.

Consider that adding zero makes no change and adding one is merely counting. Order does not matter; in addition: 8 + 5 is equal to 5 + 8. Thus a student has only 36 different single digit addition facts to learn. That includes some real toughies like 2 + 2 = 4. If the students know 8 + 5 = 13, then they also know 13 - 8 = 5 and 13 - 5 = 8. Once students memorize their addition facts, they know their subtraction facts because it is backward addition.

Multiplication by zero is zero, multiplication by one makes no change, and multiplication by two is the same as adding two like numbers. Order does not matter; 8 X 5 is the same as 5 X 8. That means there are only 28 single digit multiplication facts to learn. If you know 5 X 8 = 40, you also know 40 ÷ 5 = 8 and 40 ÷ 8 = 5. *That leaves only 64 different facts students must move into long term memory to become competent in basic arithmetic.* Our children don't learn these few facts because our elementary schools are too busy trying to teach other topics.

To truly learn something well, a student must write it and say it (recitation) day after day, year after year, until it is firmly placed in long-term memory. Repetition, recitation, and memorization all seem to be bad words in our elementary schools. Classes are supposed to be doing something fun or interesting so students learn in spite of themselves. Our brighter students can get by in this kind of environment, but even they are coming up short in their knowledge of the basics.

When we walk by elementary classes, we should hear them reciting their arithmetic facts. Teachers should be using flashcards. Those workbook pages full of practice problems may be out of style, but they are essential for moving knowledge into long-term memory. There should be timed tests requiring students to know their facts instead of using the counting method.

Your child may be receiving "A" grades in math while adding by counting and not knowing all of his or her multiplication facts. Give your child a quick verbal test. If your child can't come up with immediate responses to simple arithmetic questions, you may have to augment your school's inadequate attempt to teach the basics.

A good old fashioned thing you can do to help your child learn arithmetic is to obtain some flashcards. Use them for short periods of time, but on a regular basis. If the child gives the wrong answer or hesitates, call timeout and have the child repeat the fact out loud a time or two. Keep the facts the child misses aside and after you go through all the facts, go through ones that were missed. Keep doing this until the correct answer to each fact has been quickly given at least once. Try recording the amount of time used in each session and have a quicker time as a goal for the next session. When your child can zip through the cards in record time, you can cut down on the numbers of sessions, but don't quit. Try the flash cards every once in a while all the way through elementary school.

The nation knows that our public schools are not taking the time to do a good job with the basics so there are all kinds of ways to help you take up the slack. There are Internet Apps and programs, computer CDs, DVDs, and books. If you don't have easy access to the Internet or money for books, there is always the public library. The science behind most of these programs is that they provide the amount of practice necessary for children to remember facts and procedures.

Better programs should be in the making. Computers have already progressed to voice input. If an arithmetic fact appeared on a computer screen and had to be answered immediately by voice, the computer could take the place of teachers and parents that are too busy to use recitation and flashcards. The computer could be programmed to stress the toughest facts and could emphasize the facts most often missed. It can record total times and provide reward responses. Computers and the Internet cannot do a better job educating than good teachers in good schools. Unless our schools get back to the basics you may see more and more children staying home to be trained in this manner.

The Mathematical Sciences Education Board recommends that the curriculum for middle school should focus "on mathematics for everyday life, a theme rich in motivation that leads naturally to many important mathematical topics." This sounds reasonable, but in actual practice the overburdening of the curriculum continues.

Why does 3 + 2 equal 2 + 3? Obviously, this is true because they both add up to five. In modern math we can't just accept this fact and go on; we have to study it and give it a name—the Commutative Property. The truth is most teachers do not understand the significance of the commutative property in the development of a mathematical system. It might be difficult for some of our math teachers to come up with a good explanation. No one but a college professor would consider this mathematics for everyday life.

Schools continue trying to teach concepts previously taught in high school or college to students in middle school. They hope it will result in higher scores on state tests and college entrance exams. Meanwhile, the students add and subtract by counting, are unsure of their multiplication facts, and can't do a long division problem. Long division does take a long time and is one reason I use a calculator. However, I can still do long division because I used and reused the process while I was in elementary school. Learning long division is the culmination of the arithmetic process. It uses all the arithmetic skills including estimation. It forces facts into long term memory; it demonstrates a procedural approach to a problem.

Middle school students should have a good understanding of how money is used in our society. They should be well versed in the practical use of measurement, which means they should be learning our system as well as the metric system. Students should demonstrate skill in fractions, decimals, and percent. Everyone agrees middle school students should master the mathematics of everyday life, but instead they are fed a mixed bag of higher math concepts.

The inability to use applied arithmetic is a lifelong handicap and a constant limitation in math class. It is my contention that a ninth grader with good arithmetic skills and a knowledge of practical math will perform at a higher level in algebra class than an equally intelligent student with poor skills—despite the latter's pre-exposure to algebra concepts. Good arithmetic skills do more toward the ability to use higher mathematics than repeated attempts to teach concepts to students that are *not* ready for them.

CALCULATORS

What did our educational leaders do to compensate for our students' current deficiencies in arithmetic? They gave them calculators! I have a lesson plan for second grade with the objective of teaching how to use a calculator. Why! Provide an older child that has mastered basic arithmetic with a calculator and you won't have to teach them how to use it. Second graders might better be using that time to practice their arithmetic. Such early use of calculators is one reason they don't learn arithmetic facts. Why bother if you can count on your fingers or use a calculator?

A calculator is only correct if you use it correctly. You can push the wrong button, push it twice instead of once, not push it at all, push two buttons at once, or forget to push an operation button. They all result in the wrong answer. Students with good arithmetic skills can often do problems faster and more accurately in their heads or with pencil and paper than they can punch them into a calculator.

High school students that take the prestigious SAT college entrance test are allowed to use a calculator, but the test makers recommend that students do not use calculators for all computations. They realize that doing basic computations with a calculator takes more time than doing them mentally. Students competent in mental arithmetic definitely have an advantage when they take the timed SAT.

Students in elementary and middle school should *not* be using calculators—they should be practicing their arithmetic. When schools allow the use of calculators at early levels it sends the message that arithmetic is not important, but we know that's not true. Ask your school's principal and school board to eliminate the use of calculators in elementary and middle school. Explain to them that your child needs to practice arithmetic to place it in long-term memory.

CALCULATORS VS SPELLING MACHINES

Let's go off on a little tangent and consider the importance of spelling. The unabridged dictionary used for the national spelling bee contains over 400,000 words. *Newsweek* ran an article entitled "Can't Spell? Yur Not Dumm" (June 1988, p.52) that indicated poor spellers might have a mild form of dyslexia. It pointed out that our language comes from many sources, and phonics rules do not always apply. On top of that, our language is constantly changing. It goes on to state that it is generally accepted that poor spelling does not indicate a lack of intelligence, nor does it correlate with writing ability. For example, the famous author F. Scott Fitzgerald was a notoriously poor speller.

The time may come when a student with good arithmetic skills sues the SAT for the right to use an electronic spelling machine on the SAT writing test. A poor speller will be penalized on that tests while someone that is poor in arithmetic will have the advantage of a calculator on the math test. It is blatant prejudice to allow a student that cannot learn sixty-four math facts and a few unchanging procedures to use a machine, while a person that cannot remember how to spell some of the thousands of words in a complex, changing language is denied access to the same sort of technology.

We don't want machines robbing lower-level students of the practice needed to learn the basics. However, when students reach the high school level, we might as well give them calculators and spelling machines. If they haven't learned arithmetic and spelling by then, they probably won't learn them and those machines will help them continue their education.

SCIENTIFIC CALCULATORS

Although schools are eager to hand out simple calculators to everyone, they may come up short in the use of special calculators. When I was in college, you saw the budding young engineers running around the campus with slide rules dangling from their belts. Now they carry multifunction scientific calculators. These calculators do amazing things that only mathematicians and scientists care about, but the application of science is certainly important to our civilization. The use of scientific calculators should be part of the senior high math and science curriculum of your school. Tests should have "use your calculator" sections with questions that require many steps and difficult computations, for they are closer to the realities faced by engineers and scientists.

Parents with children that do well in math and science should inquire about their school's training in the use of scientific calculators. School officials and politicians are more likely to spend a thousand dollars on one computer than on twenty scientific calculators because anyone can use the computer, but scientific calculators are for a specialized group of individuals. Parents may have to purchase their budding scientist or engineer an appropriate calculator. Make sure it comes with a set of directions that is clear and complete so your child can teach him/herself.

"WHY JOHNNY CAN'T READ"

Rudolf Flesch, in his book on the teaching of reading *Why Johnny Still Can't Read: And What You Can Do About It*, (New York: Harper & Row, 1981, p. 4) sees a big problem with the teaching of reading in our schools. Children are taught to recognize whole words and phrases by the use of repetition.

See Sydney run.

See Kelsey run.

See Buddy run.

The recognition system is fast, but leads to errors and poor spelling. There is a big difference between a person being conscious or conscientious. The rapid reader will often use context to pick the right word and consequently may not see the individual letters that form the word. One would use this method if skimming through material searching for pertinent information. Once the information is reached it calls for more careful reading. A math question requires careful scrutiny of every word and punctuation mark. Students should learn to function at all three levels.

PHONICS

Mr. Flesch says that children need to learn the twenty-six letters of the alphabet, the forty-some sounds they can express, and know the rules that apply to their use. It is called phonics and has been ignored by our schools. He says phonics is the basis of the formation of our language and it is a proven fact that children that learn phonics are better readers and spellers.

Parents may have to take it upon themselves to teach their children phonics. You should start before they go to school and continue through the first few grades. Materials are readily available in stores and online. It certainly wouldn't hurt to cover phonics rules with struggling older readers and writers.

No matter the method, parents should encourage their children to read and write. Provide them with reading materials that hold their interest. Have young children read out loud. Silent reading is for those whose abilities have reached the point where their mind works faster than their mouths. As children mature a fiction series like Harry Potter or the classic Nancy Drew are a couple of the many possibilities. Magazines and catalogs related to their hobbies require reading. Encourage them to write thank you notes the old fashion way. Texting is well on its way to destroying the ability to write. If you can't read what your children write, you may have to teach penmanship, which is also losing ground to other curriculum. Mistakes due to poor penmanship cost businesses money, result in undelivered mail, and may result in a medical error. Who knows, our schools may eventually give up cursive writing completely and teach only printing.

References to the importance of the three R's (reading, writing and arithmetic) go back centuries. However, there have also been "learned" men who saw the time spent practicing the basics as drudgery. They are like the football player that complains about running too many wind sprints in practice, but does well in the last quarter of the game. It takes time and effort to build physical skills; it takes time and effort to push the basics into long term memory. There are a host of things a child would rather do than practice the basics. It takes compassionate, unrelenting adults to see that it gets done. If the school won't do it—you may have to take up the slack.

CHAPTER 5

INAPPROPRIATE CURRICULUM

COMMON CORE STATE STANDARDS

The latest major happening in curriculum is the implementation of Common Core State Standards into 45 states. It was completed in 2010 by the National Governors Association and the Council of Chief State School Officers. It is endorsed and supported by the federal government through "Race to the Top" grants. It seems more and more common for we ordinary citizens wake up in the morning faced with something new that will change our lives. The trouble with leaders is that they feel compelled to make changes and there is a tendency to assume that old ways are bad and new ways are good. We know that's not necessarily true.

There is no doubt that a common core curriculum is a good idea. The curriculum in the first eight grades of our public schools has been so vague and so poorly administered that our public school students ended up with totally different backgrounds. You can imagine how it varied from school to school, town to town, city to city, and state to state. It makes sense that mobile children should end up in a new class that is similar to the one they left.

Back in 1986 Dr. E. D. Hirsch Jr. founded the Core Knowledge Foundation, which has been striving toward a common core curriculum. That goal is being reached, but Dr. Hirsch has issues with the current education establishment. He says that the changes to education started in the early 1900s with the advent of progressive education. The traditional study of facts and skills was deemed inappropriate. It was replaced with unfocused methods, such as hands-on learning, that have robbed children of basic skills. He goes on to say these changes have obviously failed, and the continued attempts to use them are destroying our public schools. He calls it an anti-intellectual movement that uses trick phrases to convince people it is intellectual. He backs this up in a very scholarly manner.

Dr. Hirsch knew his colleagues were going to blast him. In his book *The Schools We Need: Why We Don't Have Them* (New York: Doubleday, 1996, p. 16.) he says: *"As I near the age of seventy*(now 85) *and begin to fade away like an old soldier, I am less concerned with the prospect of inevitable denunciation than with the responsibility to bear witness—if there is the slightest chance that doing so will help improve the quality and fairness of our schools."* If you want good public schools, it will pay you to listen to some old soldiers that are not afraid of the current education establishment.

A potential danger in a core curriculum for a whole country is that it could eventually delve into areas other than basic knowledge in English, math, science, and history. It could be used to rewrite history. It could be used to test social theories or promote a certain kind of student rather than a skilled student. What is considered basic education must be open to the scrutiny of the majority or special interest groups could use it to advance their agendas. It could be a "big brother is watching you" tool used by government to destroy individual rights and privacy.

COMMON CORE MATH

It makes sense that a child that moves should end up in a new class that is similar to the one they left, but doesn't make sense to force a curriculum on everyone that has driven the USA far down the lists of international academic achievement. We are particularly poor in math.

http://www.guardian.co.uk/news/datablog/2010/dec/07/world-education-rankings-maths-science-reading

We have seen (Chap. 4) how arithmetic has taken second place to math concepts in elementary school. Students learn to add by counting and continue to add by counting. Even if students study arithmetic they do not spend enough time on it to move it into long term memory. Common Core will introduce algebra as early as the sixth grade. All middle school students will be deprived of the opportunity to thoroughly learn "living your life arithmetic." Some students will not have matured enough to handle the abstract concepts of algebra, while others will never be ready for algebra. They will learn to hate math class at age eleven.

When your child starts algebra it is a good time to obtain a good, basic business math book. Be sure it comes with answers and tests. Don't bother with one of those overpriced school textbooks. I obtained a second hand copy of Barron's E—Z Business Math for less than $10. It is supposedly for senior high, but if your child can do algebra he or she should be able to do business math. Require a certain amount of study, perhaps when they want something. You don't have to go from beginning to end. You and/or your child can pick a relevant topic and go to work. It may be good for both of you. Your child's venture into the world of practical math could make the school's math easier.

When I started teaching the better math students took a course in algebra in ninth grade, while other students took a general math or a business math course. Now EVERY student must take a course in algebra. Think about the math you use at home and at work. Most people use arithmetic, but very few people use algebra. How much of your high school math to you remember? Do you think it is necessary that every student pass a year long course in algebra? This obsession with algebra is just one more bit of evidence that our education leaders are out of touch with the real world

Let me provide a short synopsis of what happened during my years as a math teacher. First, New York State eliminated the math courses named Algebra, Plane Geometry, Intermediate Algebra, Trigonometry, and Solid Geometry. They deleted solid geometry completely and a great deal of traditional geometry. They rearranged and overlapped the other courses and named them Ninth, Tenth, and Eleventh Year Mathematics. Some twenty years, later they threw in some new topics like probability, statistics, and number theory—mixed it all thoroughly—and named it Sequential Math. As you might guess, it was anything but sequential. Students bounced back and forth from one major topic to another for three years. It seemed to be designed to keep all but the very best of students from developing a good understanding of high school mathematics.

The state education department has to have something to do so they have circled back to the original sounding names, Integrated Algebra, Geometry and Algebra 2 with Trigonometry, but it is the same old hodgepodge that emphasizes why instead of how. Nothing about New York State's curriculum or SAT scores shows that NYS is anything more than a mediocre math achievement state in a mediocre math achievement country. However, it is this kind of curriculum that is being forced on many states because it is used in Common Core.

Algebra is to higher mathematics as arithmetic is to practical math—it is basic. Students are frustrated when they know how to do a practical problem and make an arithmetic error. They are more disheartened when they know how to solve an advanced math problem and make an algebra error. Algebra relates to all other high school math and thus a sound algebra background makes the study of those topics all the easier. It doesn't make sense to present such an important topic in a hodgepodge curriculum.

If an upper high school math teacher has students with good algebra skills, topics like sequences and series, vectors, analytic geometry, trigonometry, and calculus can be taught quickly and effectively. The students will have studied algebra long enough to store the essentials of algebra in long-term memory. They will not make basic mistakes, and the teacher will not have to use precious time going back to review algebra.

If your child likes math and is forced into a sequential math curriculum it could be advantageous to supplement it with a pure algebra course that includes all of high school algebra. If you get a book you will need an answer key and possibly solutions. Computer programs and tutors typically come with answers. Bright, engaged students can learn a great deal by themselves. Engaging a tutor if they hit a snag could be well worth the investment. Mastering algebra will put them one up on those that rely on Common Core. I ran across the following links, but you should do your own searching.

http://math.about.com/od/booksresourcesdvds/tp/algebra1.htm

http://saxonpublishers.hmhco.com/en/sxnm_home.htm

http://algebra-software-review.toptenreviews.com/

http://www.wyzant.com/TutorSearchNew.aspx?d=40&z=27850

If your child doesn't like math and is stuck in a Common Core math courses there is nothing she/he can do but try their best. Help from a friend, parent or tutor is in order. It's a crime they can't take a course in school more suited to their needs and aspirations.

SHOULD EVERYONE BE A MATHEMATICIAN?

In 1957, the Russians launched Sputnik, the earth's first man-made satellite. It appeared we were technologically behind the times and a great deal of emphasis was placed on math and science. That was good! The problem was that educators overdid it and tried to make everyone a mathematician. That was bad!

A mathematical system starts with a few postulates that are accepted without proof. The mathematician, using an accepted form of reason, proves as many conclusions as possible. The system and its conclusions need not fit any known physical model. To the mathematician the system is like a work of art. To many people it looks like spilled paint.

If it were not for the fact that mathematics ends up having many practical applications, very few people would bother with its study. The great mathematician and philosopher Bertrand Russell said, "Mathematics may be defined as the subject in which we never know what we are talking about nor whether what we are saying is true." How many people can, or care to, deal with something like that? Few people are interested in mathematical theory, proof, and the derivation of formulas. Engineers worry little about why—they want to know how.

You don't have to know the intricacies of an automatic transmission to drive a car. You certainly don't need to know the laws of physics that underlie a car's existence. Most people feel the same way about math. They want to learn a process that will provide them with an answer to a realistic problem. They are not concerned with why it works or how lovely a system it represents. Trying to teach the why of mathematics to 100% of the student body is absurd. Schools need to be flexible enough to challenge the gifted with "the why," while teaching the remainder what they want to know—how to obtain answers to practical problems.

This overemphasis on advanced mathematics for the masses is illustrative of all facets of the curriculum. From science to athletics, the proponents of each field want more students spending more time in their particular discipline. It means more jobs, more money, and more prestige for everyone in that field.

COMMON CORE LITERATURE

Not that long ago I read the recently published fiction book my seventh grade granddaughter was reading for English. It graphically described people dying in war, passively accepted drunkenness, and used swear words (and I don't mean hell and damn). This may reflect real life, but the book would have been just as interesting without resorting to shock tactics. I don't see why seventh graders need to read questionable material in school. I have seen a high school teacher fired for allowing students to read such language in class. It was a little late for me to worry about my granddaughter reading that book. I found out she had been assigned the same book when she was in fifth grade.

William Kilpatrick's in his book *Why Johnny Can't Tell Right from Wrong: Moral Illiteracy and the Case for Character Education* (New York: Simon & Schuster, 1992) maintains that children need to learn about character from their parents, their religion, and from heroes in literature. His book provides a *Guide to Great Books for Children and Teens*. What is considered great literature may be in the eye of the beholder, but schools should be very careful in their selections.

Common Core deems that nonfiction is also literature and recommends that students be assigned nonfiction works 20% of the time in lower grades and up to 70% for seniors. Some of the recommendations at the higher level are current government publications such as *U.S. General Services Administration. Executive Order 13423: Strengthening Federal Environmental,*

Energy, and Transportation Management. Is such reading education or is it indoctrination? All student texts are (or should be) nonfiction. Directions for assembly of a device or the rules of a game are nonfiction. Nonfiction is everywhere. Should English class pile on even more nonfiction?

The education elite say they want to encourage creativity, but they legislate fact gathering and opinion. One might say that opinion is creative because the same facts sometimes result in totally different opinions. Labeling theories as theories and nonpartisan comparison of disagreeing opinions should be part of every subject. On the other hand, English literature should be a showcase of the creative rather than of information and opinions. You may want to supplement what your school calls literature.

Unwise legislators succumb to the pressures of special interest groups and pass laws to support their demands. The education hierarchy doesn't mind because it also adds to their domain. Campaigns of special interest groups have resulted in curriculum that has our children studying the wrong things at the wrong time, which denies them the opportunity to thoroughly learn the basics. Is it any wonder homeschooling and private schools are flourishing?

CULTURAL CURRICULUM

The culture of the time has great impact on the education of the time. We have seen great changes in both during the last fifty years. Sadly, they both seem to be going downhill. Movies and TV shows promote sex to the point that it rivals pornography and there is an unending stream of violence. At one time gross talk and gross behavior were associated with gross people, but now it is becoming the norm. It's hard to find a news reporter anymore; they are all analysts that spin the news one way or another to support their personal views. At the same time our schools have slipped down into mediocrity when compared to other nations.

Psychologists introduced one of their more destructive theories into our schools in the 60's. The idea was that students should decide for themselves what is right and what is wrong. Students are encouraged to disregard parents, religion, history, and culture. Schools couldn't teach established morality because they would have to choose whose morality to teach. It is up to the individual to choose what is best for him or her. It seems that schools are happy to teach other cultures, but shun our own. They emphasize group study, but pile morality on the shoulders of the individual.

Though public schools don't usually teach courses called "self-morality," they do teach sex education, drug education, and life-skills education using the "self theory." Helping children deal with "living your life" problems seems like a wonderful goal, but your school's presentations could be destroying moral virtues that you have tried to instill in your child.

SEX EDUCATION

Sex education stripped of morality concentrates on the mechanics. How to have safe sex is a major topic. Condoms are introduced, and depending on the training and the whims of the instructor, various sexual situations are introduced. For instance, girls have been required to properly place condoms over boys' fingers. Of course, it is mentioned there is no such thing as absolutely safe sex. However, the basic message is that the decision is totally yours, we expect you to have sex, and this is the safe way. It might better be called sex encouragement class. The curriculum may also cover masturbation, oral sex, and homosexual activity in graphic detail.

The Mayo Clinic recommends that parents should not leave sex education totally to the school. Parent's views are important to their children. What kind of sex education do you want your child to receive in school? Many parents want personal character and abstinence to be encouraged. They want romance, love, and marriage to be extolled as the proper introduction to sex. They don't want their school age children exposed to the intimate details of unnatural sex (natural sex being stringently defined as sex that can propagate the species.) If you're one of these parents, you had better investigate your school's sex education. Many parents have done so and didn't like the results; this is one of the reasons their children attend a private school or study at home. One wonders if public schools should even teach lengthy courses in sex education.

A good public school should be happy to provide you with a detailed sex education curriculum and teach it only with your permission. Some education programs, including Sex Respect, AANCHOR, Responsible Sexual Values Program (RSVP), Me, My World, My Future, and Sexuality, Commitment and Family promote abstinence-based sex education.

DRUG EDUCATION

Psychologists also developed the most prominent drug education programs. They encouraged self-expression and self-decision making. The idea is that children shouldn't listen to their parents, their church, or the wishes of their society. They have to choose for themselves. Exposed to this "if it feels all right to you, it's OK" dogma, more and more students chose to use drugs. QUEST was one of the biggest and worse offenders and its failures promoted the government to force it to change its ways. It is still "self" centered. The DARE program is good because it uses policemen as presenters, but it is also based on the "self" approach. These programs are prominent, but not necessarily the worst or the best. A great deal of their effectiveness depends upon the teacher. All too often, programs with the potential to do more harm than good are turned over to a young, inexperienced teacher and forgotten. Don't be afraid to call your school's principal and ask detailed questions. At what grade level is drug education taught? What is the name of the program? Who teaches it? Would you send me a detailed account of what is taught? Check to see if it emphasizes the dangers of not knowing what you're getting when you obtain illegal drugs. There are also the dangers of dealing with criminals, death by drug overdose, and people that might drug you without your knowledge.

Your concern about sex and drug education will force the principal to be concerned. Check out drug and sex education classes with your child to see if the teacher is following the curriculum presented to you. Be suspicious of words like value neutral, holistic, humanistic, decision making, awareness of sexuality, and responsible sex. See how the administrator and teacher respond to words like character, virtue, and abstinence. If they give you the runaround or you are otherwise dissatisfied, take your concerns to a board member.

Much of the preceding is supported by William Kilpatrick's book *Why Johnny Can't Tell Right from Wrong: Moral Illiteracy and the Case for Character Education* (New York: Simon & Schuster), 1992, p. 71. He posed this question to both parents and teachers:

Suppose your child's school was instituting a course or curriculum in moral education at the fifth- to seventh-grade level. As a parent which of the two models below would you prefer the school use?

(A) The first approach encourages students to develop their own values and value systems. This approach relies on presenting

the students with provocative ethical dilemmas and encouraging open discussion and exchange of opinion. The ground rule for discussion is that there are no right or wrong answers. Each student must decide for himself/ herself what is right or wrong. Students are encouraged to be nonjudgmental about values that differ from their own.

(B) The second approach involves a conscious effort to teach specific virtues and character traits such as courage, justice, self-control, honesty, responsibility, charity, obedience to lawful authority, etc. These concepts are introduced and explained and then illustrated by memorable examples from history, literature, and current events. The teacher expresses a strong belief in the importance of these virtues and encourages his/her students to practice them in their own lives.

It turned out that the vast majority of parents chose B, while teachers chose A. Parents probably pick B because they are concerned about their children and are in touch with the real world. Teachers probably pick A because colleges have indoctrinated them with the idea that it is wrong to teach morality and character.

People are not innately good, and children must be taught basic moral behavior. On their own, children sometimes learn uncivilized values such as prejudice. This is all the more reason for schools to teach morality. Who would disagree with accepting honesty, reliability, fairness, self-discipline, respect for others, and the courage to live up to these ideals as positive characteristics? There is no reason that lessons in morality consistent with the views of the majority can't be taught in our elementary schools.

BAD PSYCHOLOGY VS GOOD PSYCHOLOGY

Conceivably, attempts to change our lives and schools are promoted by greedy psychologists that see new child rearing theories and the invention of more disorders as a means of making money. Parents beware! Psychology is still more philosophy than science. We must view anything psychologists say with a degree of skepticism. As parents, we have the right and the responsibility of choosing the "school of thought" that will be followed when raising our children. If you are helping your child build character, you must concern yourself with the possibility of a group of psychologists using your school to destroy your work.

You might think I don't have much time for psychologists, but that's not true. Some psychologists make a lot of sense. The early works of Dr. Wayne Dyer encouraged people to take charge of their lives and not to blame others for their failures. His later work seems more evangelical than educational.

Dr. Laurence Steinberg, an expert on child development, blames changes in society and in family life for the decline of student achievement. He explains why children from authoritarian households, which also provide emotional support, have the best chance of succeeding in our public schools.

John Rosemond is a family psychologist who says there is no proof that Attention Deficit Disorder (ADD) is a disease or genetic disorder, but rather a personality trait. Hyperactivity has been added to form a bigger and more inclusive ADHD. He regards efforts to develop a disease that may not exist as a disservice to those involved. His advice on child rearing seems to be down-to-earth and logical.

ENGLISH IS THE MOST IMPORTANT SUBJECT

American English has evolved from a multitude of cultures and is very complex. Though our hodgepodge language is difficult to master, its importance to the survival of individuals in our society cannot be denied. While striving to insure all students learn English to the best of their ability, we must face the fact people have varying ability levels. Some can readily learn several languages while others never become proficient in their own language.

Elementary classrooms should be emphasizing reading and writing. When students leave the elementary classrooms, and we begin sending them to classes taught by different teachers, two of these classes should be in English. One class should emphasize writing and speaking, and the other reading and listening comprehension.

High schools often attempt to provide special help for students at the lower end of the scale, extra work for those at the higher end of the scale, while ignoring students that *get along*, but are obviously deficient in English. These students may take remediation courses in college, but they are more apt to spend their lifetime handicapped by their inadequacies in English. Remedial help in our language should be available to every needful student at every grade level. Success in academic study or in life depends greatly upon the person's ability to read and/or write English. Let your school administrators know that you want them to emphasize English. We cannot let other aspects of the curriculum subvert its importance.

BILINGUAL EDUCATION

Should public school curriculum be taught in several languages? Bilingual education is the teaching of minority students in their own language, while gradually bringing them to an accepted level of competence in English. There are also two-way bilingual programs where the class is made up of English speaking students and students speaking another language. The goal is student proficiency in both languages.

My *World Almanac* tells me there are 220 different languages that have at least one million speakers. Should our public schools be prepared to provide bilingual education for 220 different languages? Perhaps we should have "bicent-lingual" education where students become proficient in 200 languages. Obviously, both ideas are ridiculous. We propose to be an equal opportunity nation, but when we provide a major minority with a special curriculum in a bilingual classroom, we are discriminating against the many other minorities that are also Americans. Our schools are staffed with experts in various fields. We cannot expect all teachers to know all languages. Thus, to make this expertise available to all children, all of our students must know our form of English as soon as possible.

Even the writers of the Bible considered different languages a handicap to mankind. Genesis 11:9 reads "That is why the city was called Babel (meaning confusion), because it was there that Jehovah confused them by giving them many languages, thus widely scattering them across the face of the earth."

It would be foolish to bury our heads in the sand and ignore the existence of hundreds of other languages. Exposing elementary students to several other languages and cultures makes a lot of sense. It would be great if they could say a few key words and phrases from the lineage of members of the class. It is not the time for public schools to try to make them fluent in two languages.

MULTICULTURALISM

Multicultural education has the same problem as bilingual education; there are too many cultures represented in the USA to properly cover them all. Students should realize there are many people with customs and beliefs that are different then their own, but featuring one of those cultures is a disservice to the others.

The USA is known as the "great melting pot," where people of all races and creeds blend together. The theory behind multicultural education is that it teaches people of different cultures to get along with one another. Pride in one's heritage can be comforting, but excessive cultural pride can result in self-segregation, gangs, violence, and all-out war. We see culturally opposed groups at war throughout the world, especially in Afghanistan and Iraq. The USSR controlled ethnic violence within its borders for many years. When it fell, many of these groups went right back to war. It got so bad that we intervened in Kosavo. Could multiculturalism actually retard rather than enhance the melting pot process?

Difficulties occur when we begin making controversial cultural interpretations about the past. Which group was right? Which one was wrong? Who is vindicated? Who was maltreated? We must realize that humanity has yet to evolve out of savage-like behavior and what has happened cannot be changed. Becoming embroiled in an analysis of the past that drives people apart is self destructive. This is particularly true when schools involve themselves in such nebulous areas as politics and religion. Let's leave interpretation to the intellectuals that seem to have nothing better to do. Let those people in school know you want them to teach knowledge and skills rather than trying to interpret the world's cultures. The right to cultural instruction belongs to parents!

CHILD CENTERED SCHOOLS

One of the currently touted education theories is that teachers should be merely guides that help students discover knowledge in which they are interested. This might work in the confines of home schooling, but a public school class needs a trail boss. Catering to the whims and interests of twenty or more students is impossible and trying to do so has to take away from the learning of basic skills. Tell those people in school to hire teachers—not mere facilitators.

HOMOGENEOUS VS HETEROGENEOUS GROUPING

When I went to high school, it was common to see students of similar abilities placed in the same classroom, and it is named Homogeneous Grouping. The current trend is to put all ability levels in the same classroom, and it is named Heterogeneous Grouping. It seems logical that students should go to classes best suited to their abilities and needs. However, many of our modern educators claim students in lower tracts do not try and being in class with the best students can be a boost to them. Good students could help lift the poor students, but on the other side of the coin, the poor students could pull down the good students. Teachers that spend part of their time challenging the best students and part of their time on remediation of the poorest students are not serving either group adequately. The "everyone can do it" theory is beautiful; the ugly fact is that we are created with differing abilities.

Some students excel in all areas, and we must train them well because they are the great doers and leaders of tomorrow. Other students excel in a few areas, show competence in some areas, and need remediation in a subject or two. It makes sense to put them in classes that challenge them in areas where they excel and provide remediation in areas where they are weak. The needs of every student should be evaluated and a schedule built that will allow them to attend college entrance courses in some subjects while attending lower-level and/or remedial courses in others. That is not easy to do! When counselors and administrators say mixed grouping is best, they might be less than honest. The underlying factor could be that it is much easier for them to simply throw all ability levels into one classroom. Parents should lobby for classes that fit their child's needs rather than having them suffer through "one-class-fits-all."

CURRICULUM COORDINATORS

If there are problems with curriculum it is not because it is ignored. A school system of any size has a curriculum coordinator, perhaps designated in another way such as Director of Instruction. As the system gets bigger there will be more than one, perhaps one for elementary and one for secondary. The system may go so far as to hire one for a particular subject such as math. They will have a certificate or a special degree or even a doctorate. They work out of the administrative office, report to the superintendent's office and are paid administrative wages. They also deal with other curriculum people that work for the state or for the federal government. They are college people, trained by college people and they work with college people. It is obvious that their primary goal is to place as many children in college as possible. The college crowd has everyone believing that college is the answer to everything. Consequently, we have too many college graduates that have accumulated large debts and can't find appropriate jobs.

I applied for a curriculum coordinator position once and here is part of my letter. *My primary credentials for curriculum coordinator are based on experience, not education. I see curriculum study taking place in three stages. The first stage would be information gathering. This would involve visiting classes, talking with faculty and administration, and receiving written input from everyone involved. The second stage would be analyzing data, pinpointing problems, and developing possible solutions. The third stage would be the adoption, rejection, or modification of these proposals by the administration and staff. A school's curriculum coordinator should be willing to seek needed changes at the state level as well as the local level.*

Hire me three days a week, without benefits, for the maximum allowed by the New York State Retirement System (about

$12,000$). We would hire three other retired teachers on a two-day-a-week basis for $8,000. My primary experience is in college entrance academics, one of the others would have experience in elementary, one in the arts, one in vocational education, and I would coordinate their efforts. In forty weeks you would be getting 360 days of work from people with considerable experience and it would cost only $36,000 with no benefits. A full-timer would provide only 200 days and would undoubtedly cost much more.

My letter was sent, as instructed, to the school's superintendent. The reply was not from the superintendent, but rather from the principal of the high school. He indicated that he was about to retire, and it would take some time to hire a replacement. Since the high school principal would have a great deal of involvement with the new curriculum coordinator, it had been decided to put off the hiring of a curriculum coordinator for one year, so the new principal could be involved in the selection.

First, this made me think the position of curriculum coordinator could not be very important. If the job could be put off one year, it could be put off two years—or perhaps indefinitely. Back in my day, teachers and administrators handled changes in state curriculum by themselves. One wonders if this position represents a legitimate need or just another addition to the non-teacher payroll.

Second, even if he thought using retired teachers was a good idea, no superintendent would dare implement the plan. The education hierarchy wants to expand and the colleges that grant graduate degrees find this a great way to make money. My suspicions were confirmed one year later when the same job was advertised again with the addition of the sentence "Administrative certification is preferred."

Third, curriculum coordinators are not supposed to work with teachers and challenge the education hierarchy—they tell teachers what to teach as assigned from above. Most people would agree coordinating the efforts of others in endeavors such as sports and musical presentations requires someone with experience and talent in that profession. We wouldn't require a coach or a musical conductor to have a master's degree in business administration. However, the education hierarchy wants us to believe someone who studies administration in college is better prepared to deal with curriculum than experienced teachers. I contend that twenty or more years of successful teaching is much better training for curriculum development than two years worth of college courses. There have been some strong-willed teachers, such as John Saxon who wrote his own series of math textbooks to challenge the education establishment, but the "powers-that-be" do their best to isolate him.

TEXTBOOKS

A good text is essential to both student and teacher, but your child may not have textbooks appropriate to the curriculum. It seems that texts published by the big companies are either written or edited by college professors. The authors of math texts place a great deal of emphasis on mathematical theory, but examples of problem solutions tend to be scarce and poorly written. Too many school texts are hard to read and have a mishmash of student exercises. Some are accompanied by tests that do not properly correspond to the text. Some seem to represent the disjointed efforts of several people. Some have come under fire for promoting an agenda rather than facts.

There are many experienced teachers who could write good textbooks, but the textbook companies put their stock in college people. Professors cannot meet the needs of teachers and students because they are not familiar with those needs. College writers are more interested in building a book acceptable to their peers than educating public schoolchildren. Publishers should get rid of those college professor writers and editors, and replace them with master teachers. Then our children could work with decent textbooks.

I wrote for some sample copies of Mr. Saxon's teacher produced texts, but the reply to my request was that the content would not fit the curriculum of New York State. The reason is that Mr. Saxon's texts stress drill and practice with a gradual introduction of new topics, while the state stresses theory and quickly introduces a multitude of concepts. Could it be that Mr. Saxon knows more about the educational needs of children than the hierarchy of New York State?

VOCATIONAL CURRICULUM

Another failing of our public schools is the theory that all students must study a curriculum oriented toward college. President Bush concurred with the No Child Left Behind Act. President Obama, in his 2012 budget, proposed a 20 percent reduction for technical education while seeking an 11 percent overall increase in the education budget. If schools truly cared about their clientele, they would take a good, honest look at the capabilities and needs of students. We have to admit there are young teenagers who hate school. They tend to miss many days of school, and then they drop out at as soon as they are sixteen. It is a shame, but 25% of our students do not graduate from high school.

Vocational training has not disappeared, but it suffers. In New York State there is the Board of Cooperative Educational Services (BOCES). It provides vocational education for junior and senior students. They are bused to a central location for half a day to take courses like auto mechanics, cooking, cosmetology, secretarial, etc. By the time schools bus a seventeen or eighteen-year-old off to

BOCES for a couple of hours and then back to captivity, the time to work with them is minimal, and so are the results.

We should make trade training available to academically disadvantaged students in their early teens and for a full day. Some will say that children in their early teens are too young to be put in vocational classes because they might get hurt. They are just as apt to get hurt on the athletic field. If we can put eighth graders into algebra class we can put ninth graders into vocational activity.

Many vocational teachers are not happy with their classes. Some of their students see vocational training as a escape from regular school and are often disinterested, unreliable, and unruly. Tough discipline and a younger clientele could change that. The vocational teacher would have students that are more manageable and have more time to train them. It would certainly beat keeping them prisoners in a regular academic classroom. To someone that hates school there is a big difference between being invited to attend a class designed to help you make a living and being forced to attend a bunch of classes aimed at college entrance.

If the vocationally inclined could go to an all-day vocational school at the ninth grade level, academically poor students would be provided with a realistic educational goal of getting through the eighth grade and then going to vocational school. In addition to hands-on activities, they could read, write, and do arithmetic in their chosen fields and at their own level rather than being forced into college entrance study. It would remove those students from an atmosphere they hate and place them in one they could tolerate, perhaps one where they would excel.

The students with at least two years of experience at vocational school should be released from the child labor laws so they could look for apprentice jobs with artisans. Child labor laws supposedly protect young people from unscrupulous employers and dangerous work. In reality they put sixteen-year-old dropouts into the vulnerable situation of having given up on school, but being too young to get a good job. Students that have acquired work experience and safety training at vocational school would certainly be safer working as apprentices in legitimate trades than dealing drugs on the street.

Educators at all levels, along with their allies in government have done everything they can to replace the age-old practice of apprenticeship with schooling. Laws demanding schooling rather than allowing apprenticeship cost us many education dollars while providing us with inferior products.

There is no doubt our schools serve a hierarchy of intellectuals rather than the common person. It is time we made some tangible changes in the way we deal with non-academic students and stop trying to make intellectuals out of everyone. We can best educate certain teenagers by realistically filling their needs rather than lowering our standards so everyone can be a "regular" high school graduate. Who knows? We might eventually be able to find a good electrician at a reasonable price when we need one. That electrician will be earning a good living instead of sitting in jail or living off welfare. We should all be lobbying for more public school vocational training. It would provide teenagers that hate school an alternative while allowing academic teachers to strive toward excellence instead of mediocrity.

ADVANCEMENT

My oldest granddaughter was put in the advanced math program, which meant pre-algebra in seventh grade and algebra in eighth grade. That burns me up! This advanced program will omit a great deal of basic middle school math she should have learned. Many school administrators think it looks good to have advanced programs with high enrollments, so they tend to put too many students in these programs. It is a thrill to be placed in an advanced program—a demoralizing disappointment to find it too difficult. A few children mature very quickly and apparently benefit from advancement. It is a personal matter, but I would refrain from advancing any child unless the child is some sort of genius.

David Davenport, former president of Pepperdine University, had some similar things to say: *(Cape Cod Times, August 16, 1998, p. G-7)*

"For most kids, mere acceleration of learning does not inherently enrich his or her education, and it can be counterproductive. And it may rob them of time for other kinds of experiences that would make them better adults.... I believe we have confused acceleration of learning for enrichment.... My plea to parents is this: Don't be seduced by mere acceleration."

Mr. Davenport did not come to this conclusion based on his college study or the latest education research. It was reached through his experience helping his three children through school and experience beats the heck out of education.

Schools should request parental permission to place a child in an advanced program, but if your child has high grades they might do it automatically. Call the school principal if this happens. Tell him or her that you don't like the idea of advanced programs and must be convinced before you will allow your child's participation. Don't let the school administration force your child into such a program just because they think it's a feather in their cap to have a high percentage of their students in advanced courses.

CHAPTER 6

ROBBING STUDENTS AND TEACHERS OF NEEDED CLASS TIME

ELEMENTARY INTERRUPTIONS

She was in third grade when my granddaughter was pleased to tell me, "Today in school we only had time for one short lesson all morning." Most teachers would agree that morning is the best time to teach the important subjects, and that a regular schedule is most conducive to learning. However, grade teachers seldom complain about a large number of outside classes because each of these represents a break from their classroom teaching.

Elementary school is typically in session six hours a day for 180 days. Discarding nine hours a day for sleep, each year only 20% of a child's waking time is scheduled for school. Much of that time is spent with someone other than the regular classroom teacher. There is art, physical education, library, music, and lunch. In my mother's one-room school, the teacher handled all of the above. Now we have certified specialists performing each of these duties. They are all important (especially lunch) and it certainly makes sense to have these subjects taught by experts. We are paying all these experts good money, so administrators try to keep them busy. Thus, these "special" teachers end up using too much student time and administrators allow them too much leeway in the scheduling of their classes.

It is the responsibility of the schools' administrators to insure that children have sufficient time to learn the essentials. Some administrators not only fail to do their jobs; they add to the problem. For instance, our local middle school guidance counselor advertised for volunteers to come to school to teach students about their interests and hobbies. The rationale given was that it breaks up the monotony of February and March. The children may be entertained and the presenters appreciate the opportunity to tell about their hobbies, but it is just one more in a long list of interruptions to basic instruction. Accomplished teachers don't consider long stretches of uninterrupted school days monotonous; they consider it prime teaching time.

School days are short and there are not many of them. School administrators should be determining the amount of time the elementary and middle school classes are spending on the three R's. Some activities eat up huge blocks of time, even whole school days. If students fail to use a large percent of their school time on the basics, there should be some adjustments. That could mean a cutback in time spent in special classes and on extracurricular activities. Students shouldn't have to spend the whole day with their noses in a book, but the breaks should not be lengthy. This kind of change might temporarily make some of the inhabitants of the school unhappy. However, it would result in better-prepared students entering the higher grades.

As is the case in most states, the State of New York continually adds clutter to the curriculum by requiring students study many things other than the three R's. For example, our elementary school spent a lot of time teaching bicycle safety. There was also fire education, drug education, and abduction instruction. If the public schools must take the responsibility of teaching "living-your-life" topics, it should be done in physical education class rather than during core class time. Physical education would become much more than just sports training if it had the responsibility of teaching all those physical aspects of living.

When I was a boy, our physical education was called recess and we looked forward to it as a break from the rigors of study. Asian elementary schools take several recess breaks throughout the day for children to play. In our schools, physical education can be an organized intrusion on class time that many students dread. Elementary physical education classes should be places where students can let off a little steam after a hard morning's work on the three Rs.

In addition to the many scheduled "outside" classes, there are programs, plays, and concerts to practice, perform and watch. There are parties for all occasions and field trips galore. Just before Christmas, the local shopping mall was full of young elementary students visiting Santa Claus. Christmas is wonderful, but why are we paying master's degree holders to introduce little children to Santa? The kids were having a good time, but from the point of view of a teacher, parent, and taxpayer—they should have been in school. It couldn't hurt to let school officials know that you don't like the idea of too many or too lengthy interruptions to your child's basic education. You might ask the teacher and the principal if they keep track of the amount of time actually spent on the three Rs.

SECONDARY INTERRUPTIONS

The following comes from an article in *NEA Today* entitled "If Only We Had 180 Days for Teaching," February, 1988, p. 33. *Here is a partial list of the reasons for absence [from class] recently documented by a single classroom teacher at my school:*

family vacation

counselor appointment

medical appointment

dental appointment

PSATs

ERB and EQA tests

SAT workshop

district band

band sectionals

district chorus

choral rehearsal

choral program

exchange concert

religious holiday

blood drive

tech school presentation

field trip

service club luncheon

photographs

college visitation

military scholarship interview and physical

driver training

gifted program apprenticeship

candy distribution for junior class

candy distribution for Spanish club

beginning-of-school orientation assembly

academic competition

> *in-school suspension in the principal's office*
>
> *senior trip*
>
> *chorus trip*
>
> *Europe trip*
>
> *student council meeting*
>
> *intramurals*
>
> *golf meet*
>
> *swim meet*
>
> *excused early for sports*
>
> *excused early for prom*

Did you read them all? Just the length of the list is mind-boggling. It is hard to believe this is a partial list and many high school teachers can contribute additional excuses that administrators accept for classroom absenteeism. One year my junior math class lost nine of the ninety days in the first semester for reasons similar to those above. The administration preempted 10% of my teaching time for activities they considered more important than my class. One of those activities was a writing contest sponsored by the County Principal's Association.

One of our English teachers had a similar problem: *We had a jump out the window fire drill during my eleventh grade Regents English class (which, by the way, I had to teach the last period of the day because of the vocational school's schedule) during a week wherein I already lost a class for the junior-senior picnic and part of a class due to concert practice—all during the last week of instruction before the exam."* It must have been very frustrating to have a planned week of intensive review for a statewide test ruined by forces beyond her control. Worst of all, if her students didn't do well on the test, she is the one who received the blame.

Years ago, the prevailing reason for students losing class time was illness. Extracurricular activities were conducted outside of class, and school officials accepted few excuses for student absenteeism. Things gradually changed. Being a good teacher or administrator was not enough. To make a big splash in education, you had to come up with a new club, another special field trip, or perhaps add a new sport. The newborn activity got into the school paper, the town's paper, and maybe on TV. The urge to do something special can overcome the responsibility to do what is right.

Sometimes the parents and school boards are the ones caught up in an extracurricular activities craze. Our faculty once received a letter from the school board indicating that the board considered extracurricular activities just as important as academics. When adults have that kind of attitude, how can you blame children for feeling classes are of little importance? This extracurricular blitz was a deficiency in my school and one that many others see in their schools. The problem in a giant city school system may be that there are not enough activities to involve all the students. That is one more reason to divide those huge city districts up into neighborhood schools.

Extracurricular activities have grown in importance to the point that they seem more valuable than class time. Although some teachers complain about these kinds of absences, many school administrators continue to accept them. After all, the students were to go to the teacher outside of class time and make up the work. These administrators are not experienced teachers and don't realize such meetings are difficult to schedule and a responsibility some students may not fulfill. Attending a well-managed classroom is still the best way to learn. It is likely that even those students who diligently try to make up work will not learn as much as they would have learned in class.

A host of administrative-approved student absences is the kind of school policy that robs our children and their teachers of the opportunity to achieve to their fullest. We do not necessarily need longer school days, or more school days, but we do need to insure that students are in their classrooms on a regular basis. Ask your school administrator to make this a priority.

TRIPS

School sponsored trips interfere with study all the way through high school. I'll never forget the time when my wife and I were chaperones for the senior class trip to New York City. One evening we took a group of students to a baseball game at Shea Stadium. We traveled by subway, our first experience, and just getting there was quite an adventure. On the return trip, in the middle of the night, we survived a ride in a subway car packed like a sardine can to emerge between avenues on a dark street. It was completely deserted except for the gang of about twenty young men that blocked our way. Miraculously, the leader of the gang (who spoke mostly in four letter words) passed us right through. It was sure a relief to get to the lights and crowds of Seventh Avenue. There are so many inherent dangers in trips with large groups of students that one wonders why it is even allowed.

The poorest reason in the world for sending a group of students off on a trip is that they all happen to be in the senior class. If there has to be a class trip, it should be in the lower grades where students are eager and more manageable. It is much more logical to base trips on interests rather than grade level. The orchestra should go to the philharmonic, the French club to a city with native French speakers, and the marching band to a parade.

In some schools, students and teachers spend a great deal of their time raising money to go on trips. This is a misuse of funds—taxpayers pay teachers to educate children, not to raise money to go on questionable trips on school days. Our school boards should decree that trips cannot interfere with classes, and the boards should pay for all trips. If a school trip is not worth spending the taxpayers' money, it shouldn't be taken.

ATHLETICS

Students of all our schools spend a great deal of their time as participants and as spectators at school athletic events. This is to the disgust of some academic teachers that feel all this time should be spent on study. Unlike those counterparts, I always considered school athletics very important. Our young people are physically and mentally challenged by the competition on the athletic field. They set goals and (hopefully) learn about teamwork. They compete on the athletic field rather than in the streets. Overall, sports have contributed to the stability of our society.

Of course, there are problems to be faced in the field of public school sports. Some students, even at the elementary level, get the idea that sports are more important than study. They believe they are sure to become professional athletes. Schools that fail to require superior athletes to live up to academic standards help support this belief. Coaches that are more interested in winning than in education also support this questionable goal.

Our schools should be just as interested in having good coaches as having good teachers, but we should be suspicious of coaches that always have winning teams. They could be very skilled, or they could be monopolizing student time to the detriment of the remainder of the school system. They could be using unscrupulous recruiting methods to insure they always have talented athletes. They could be so intent on winning that they teach cheating and violence. On the other hand, you have the inept coaches that cannot teach skills and lack the discipline to require teamwork. Either kind is a detriment to a child's life.

Physical education teachers are obviously the most qualified to be coaches, but they often beg off, complaining that the job requires long hours, receives little pay, and they shouldn't be asked to teach all day and coach every evening. Consequently, many schools are forced to hire coaches that have little or no training and that may not be members of the faculty. Your children may end up with coaches that can't teach skills, teamwork, and sportsmanship.

Although after-school sports may be neglected, there is overkill during school hours. Students take too many physical education classes, and physical education teachers set excessive in-school requirements. One twelve-year-old had started her menstrual cycle and wore a pad, so she brought a note to school asking that she be excused from swimming. The physical education teacher said she should be using tampons and assigned her a report as punishment. That teacher had overstepped her bounds and usurped valuable study time from the core subjects.

Our school gave number grades in physical education and required students to take long, involved written tests. I believe the main purpose was to be able to threaten unruly students with low grades rather than teach essential information. I do know it interfered with core curriculum instruction. I saw my study hall students studying the rules of volleyball and the dimensions of the volleyball court when they might better have been studying a core subject.

Public school physical education should be exercise and personal enlightenment—not a graded subject. College is the place for those interested in a physical education career to be tested on the finer points. Schools with competent administrators and physical education teachers don't need to threaten students with low marks to maintain discipline. If your school gives grades in physical education, you may be able to convince your school board to change it back to a pass/fail subject.

To properly utilize our physical education teachers, schools should change their hours to noon through evening. Gym classes would be held in the afternoon, not during the choice morning teaching time. Coaching could then become part of the physical education teacher's regular employment, which would keep those experts at the reigns of our athletic teams. Student athletes would experience the more rigorous aspects of athletic involvement, but it would not be forced on all students during the time of day they should be learning the three R's.

Reducing the number of required physical education classes while changing the working hours and responsibilities of teachers may make a lot of sense, but you and your school board would have a tough time getting it done. Many administrators and members of the education hierarchies came from the physical education field. They have worked hard to expand physical education beyond reasonable bounds. This provides more jobs for these teachers and expands the power and influence of the elite. They will fight any attempt to reduce their domain. Changing working hours and responsibilities is a change in employment and the teachers' union will fight that on principle. It will take a revolution by parents to make such changes.

TEACHER LESSON PLANS

Some schools operate under the theory that all teachers need detailed lesson plans. When I started teaching, I tried teaching from notes, but it proved unsatisfactory. It was much more effective when I reviewed the material beforehand and taught with no written plans. Would you go to a doctor or lawyer that had to constantly refer to notes or a book when discussing your problem? Teachers need a strong personality for discipline, good knowledge of their subject, the ability to communicate that knowledge, and maybe a little showmanship or humor to top it off. They don't need detailed lesson plans. Schools that require teachers construct detailed lesson plans could be wasting their teachers' time and stifling their presentations.

Some administrators claim teachers should write detailed lesson plans so their substitutes can use them. It is often difficult to find qualified substitutes. Teachers should plan ahead as to topic and assignment, and if substitutes understand the material they should teach it in their own way. If they do not understand the material, the most detailed of lesson plans would not help. The substitutes might better just give the assignment or play a DVD than confuse students by tackling something beyond their abilities.

There are rumors of teachers being provided with detailed daily lesson plans from "above" that they have to teach. If that were the case you could hire high school graduates to teach elementary school and pay them half of the current rate. We would also have to worry about the "above" having an agenda.

STUDY HALLS

In my time almost every high school teacher was responsible for a study hall. If they were not: (1) they had six or more classes; (2) they had buttered up the administration; (3) they had some other duty such as department head (number 3 often relates to number 2); or (4) they had proven so incompetent as study hall monitors that the administration avoided problems by not assigning study hall duty.

Study hall is meant to be a place where students go to study when they are not in class. In some circumstances it is a chance for teachers and students to get some work done. Under other circumstances it can be hell on earth. The best students carry a large class load and do not have many study halls. Poorer students tend to have several study halls, but one reason they are poor students is that they see study hall as a place to fool around rather than study. Chances are that many of the students in a study hall are not a bit interested in study. The teacher is functioning as a babysitter. In some cases it could be more accurately described as prison guard. This type of assignment can ruin a teacher's day, while robbing both the teacher and the more diligent students of the opportunity to get some work done.

One solution to the study hall problem is in the book *Doc: The Story of Dennis Littky and His Fight for a Better School*. Littky (Contemporary Books 1989). Mr. Littky figured out how to eliminate study halls from his school's schedule. He shortened the school day for students—not for teachers—and arranged it so that every student was in an appropriate class for the entire time they were in school. It reportedly turned the school around to a place where teachers taught and students learned. It does seem a waste of a teacher's time to baby-sit a study hall, but teacher aides are finding study hall too tough to handle. The deterioration of public school discipline is leading to the demise of study halls. It is a sad situation when schools allow a small group of undisciplined students to rob other students of the opportunity to do homework in school. Ask your child if study halls are places where he or she can study. If not, a call to the principal is in order.

HOMEROOM

Homeroom is the place where middle and high school teachers take attendance, lead the Pledge of Allegiance, and listened to announcements. It is typically of short duration and those are the only requirements, but that is not always the case. The following is a memo received by all our homeroom teachers.

HOMEROOM TEACHER RESPONSIBILITIES

In addition to regular subjects, the law requires instruction in certain special subjects. These include:

Patriotism

Citizenship

History, significance, meaning, and effect of the Constitution of the United States and amendments thereto

Constitution of New York State and amendments

Declaration of Independence

The flag

The nature and effect of alcoholic beverages

The nature and effect of narcotic and habit-forming drugs

Highway safety

Fire prevention and safety from fire hazards

Humane treatment of animals and birds

Conservation Day

Fire safety in the home and school

Bus safety

Although theoretically we were to teach all these things in homeroom, in actual practice we only taught bus safety and the homeroom period had to be lengthened (and classes shortened) to accomplish that. It is nonsensical to believe all those topics could or should be taught in a homeroom situation. That was simply the administrator's way of paying lip service to the many state laws passed by legislators trying to appease special interest groups and passing the buck on to teachers. Many of our education laws are obsolete, restrictive, biased or foolish. We obviously need to reverse the trend toward more laws and get rid of a few. If you can find them, vote for political candidates that promise to give control of schools back to the people rather than the politicians trying to control something they know nothing about.

CAFETERIA DUTY

One of the toughest obligations for teachers is cafeteria duty. The cafeteria may be full of students from different classes and of differing ages. The goal is to keep them from screaming, throwing things, making messes, or hurting one another. It is far from an educational experience, and some schools do hire non-teaching monitors. However, it is difficult to find anyone that can handle the duty effectively. School boards should require administrators to assume full responsibility for the cafeteria. If your school's principal can't keep the cafeteria under control, your school needs an administrative makeover.

A HOST OF OTHER ACTIVITIES

There is a host of extracurricular responsibilities piled on the shoulders of teachers. There are ballgames and dances to chaperone. In addition to chaperoning trips some teachers are forced to supervise moneymaking activities for a trip and may even have to be the organizer. Clubs and classes need advisers. Someone has to direct school plays. Some teachers become involved as sport coaches. Someone has to oversee the national honor society, the production of the yearbook, and the student council. All of the aforementioned duties can be very stressful and can detract from a teacher's performance. If those tasks must be done and teachers must do them, the teachers should receive appropriate additional pay for each such assignment. Schools tend to either not pay for such work or pay an inappropriately small amount. Teachers that take direct responsibility for students' activities are much more deserving of good extra pay than those sitting alone in their rooms being department heads or curriculum coordinators.

SETTING PRIORITIES

One of the major reasons your children and their teachers may be involved in too many questionable activities is that the education hierarchy believes you want it that way. Some people say, "Teachers get all that money—they ought to work hard." That is a true statement, but we pay for teachers to spend their time educating children. When other activities begin to interfere, we receive diminishing returns on our investment. Other people say, "Our children deserve every available opportunity." On the other hand, too many opportunities can be mind-boggling to the student and detract from basic learning.

The control of school activities clearly lies with school administrators. At one time they set proper priorities, but now they seem to be more interested in looking good than taking control. If concerned parents want productive schools, they may have to assume the role of the heavy and put their children and their teachers back to work in the classroom. Let your school's administrators know you expect them to shoulder more of the responsibility for how your children spend their time. Let them know your number one priority is basic classroom education. If that fails, ask members of your school board to require school administrators to set and enforce proper priorities or suffer the consequences.

This will not be an easy job for school administrators, and they will be asking themselves many questions. Will some students and their parents rebel if I reduce or cut favorite activities? Will the school board back me if the students and parents rebel? Will the winning coach leave if I cut back on the practice schedule?

The job requires people with the ability to keep everything in its proper perspective and effectively deal with the dissenters. Proper priorities may require some tough, hard decisions. We need people that can handle the job with wisdom and justice. These are attributes that colleges can't teach. They have to be learned in real-life situations. We need to empower people with experience!

You may have to assume the responsibility of limiting your child's activities. Some students can handle schedules that would dismay most adults. More power to them! However, other students are over extended. If your child's grades are suffering from too many courses or too many activities, work with them to reduce the load. In some cases it may be easy because the child is doing all these things because they feel you want them involved in everything. In other cases the mere suggestion of giving up activities because of poor grades may improve grades. When push comes to shove, it may be tough to insist that you child give up an activity, but in the long run they will appreciate your tough love.

CHAPTER 7

BEWARE OF EDUCATION INNOVATION

"Don't turn the page because there is a dirty picture and a bad word." Of course, my seventh graders would immediately turn the page, and there would be a picture labeled "protractor." To me that devise was so poorly named I placed it in the same category as a swear word; they were not to use that word in class. Pointing out its shape and the fact that no human measurement can be truly exact, it was renamed "Semi-Circular Angle Approximating Device." SCAAD was the name we used in class. They loved it, and when someone inadvertently used the P-word, it was immediately met with disapproving sounds.

Although I considered my P-word lesson successful; it had aspects that many modern educators would dislike. My students were seated at their desks, which were arranged in rows. I stood in front of the classroom and showed everyone how to use a SCAAD. Then I provided each student with a SCAAD and set him or her to work measuring angles while I wondered about the classroom, observing their individual efforts and helping when needed. This is called a traditional classroom and many of our education elite look upon it with disdain.

TRADITIONAL CLASSROOM VS GROUP STUDY

Highly placed educators are apt to tell you that students should be sitting in groups and studying in groups. The teacher should become part of the group instead of the group leader. They claim that the traditional classroom is too boring, too restrictive, and turns students off. They are apt to use derogatory terms like "factory school." This is a clever, but bogus portrayal. The real reason for the education establishment's scorn of the traditional classroom might be that our education leaders are notoriously mediocre students. College graduates applying for admission to graduate school are often required to take the Graduate Record Exam, which is similar to the SAT. The lowest average score belongs to the group going into education. Perhaps they do not like the traditional classroom because that is where the doctors, lawyers, scientists, and engineers beat them soundly in scholastic achievement. Perhaps that is why these people keep diligently trying to change our public schools.

Working with several people can be both confusing and distracting. It can also teach dependency on others. Children that constantly work with other children may end up unable to work by themselves. Elementary school is not the place for group study. Elementary students should be learning the three R's and other individual skills. Appropriate group endeavors such as band, yearbook, and sports will occur naturally in the higher grades.

If your child cannot work without someone else around or is constantly on the phone while doing homework, it is because schools emphasize group study at the expense of self-study. Ask your child if she or he sits with and communicates with other students most of the day. If this is the case, you may have to help your child develop self-study abilities. You can start by providing a private place to study. It is common for Asian parents with limited household space go to great lengths and sacrifice to provide their child with a desk and study area. If you follow their example it will provide a counterbalance to public school group-oriented activities. If you have limited resources, you can use the kitchen table; just remove the distractions. This may take a little extra effort on your part, but it will help your child develop skills your school is neglecting

My experience tells me the focused traditional classroom is still the most efficient overall approach to education, and most students appreciate a good old-fashioned lesson where they are obviously learning something. Parents with children aspiring to something higher than mediocrity should make their school more responsible. When you talk to your child's teacher, the school administrator, or school board members tell them there should be a proper balance between group study and individual study. The USA was built on individualism, not socialism. Don't let public schools squash your child's individuality.

COOPERATIVE LEARNING

Cooperative learning sounds fine if it means working together on a class project like a birthday calendar, the school yearbook, playing in the band, or being on a sports team. In a way, the traditional classroom is a cooperative effort—teacher and students are working together toward the same goal. However, modern cooperative learning may mean students of all abilities are put in groups of three to five to work on projects. Sometimes everyone in the group receives the same grade.

Supporters of modern cooperative education say that it gives the poor student a chance to contribute, but it is also apt to teach dependency and provide a false sense of accomplishment. The industrial use of teams to work on projects could be the source of this concept. People are put on industrial teams because of the skills they have demonstrated, which is a far cry from placing young schoolchildren on teams just because they are there. Individual skills such as playing an instrument must be learned before a person becomes part of a musical group. Overemphasis on cooperative learning robs both teacher and student of the time needed to insure that everyone learns basic skills.

LEARNING STYLES

Educators determined some students learn best from the discussion method, some the information method, some the coaching method, and some the discovery method. Depending on grade level and subject matter, all of these methods have their place. The discussion method may be fine for social studies class, but not for math. My courses lent themselves toward the information and coaching methods. Science labs emphasize the discovery method, but students still have to go to science class because there is just too much to learn to rediscover it all.

As usual, the armchair educators got carried away and advocated that teachers adjust their teaching to fit their student's favorite learning method. This is obviously impractical! If teachers have a class of any size, all four preferences will be present and they certainly cannot take the time to teach everything four different ways. Teachers develop their methods by experience and use the method or combination of methods that seems to work best for the topic, the students, and themselves. It is the students that must develop the ability to learn from all four methods. When they go to college or out on the job, they are not going to have a choice as to how they are trained.

MASTERY TEACHING

Mastery teaching requires every student to master every part of the curriculum. It sounds demanding, but it is just an alternate to group testing as a means of checking student progress. For example, if an elementary student can pass three tests on multiplication by four, she or he can mark it off on the chart and then work on some sort of enrichment until everyone in class has completed the task.

Then they move on to multiplication by five. Almost any student can retain a small group of facts for a short period of time. Mastery teaching should be considered the "at least they knew it once" technique. If your child's school uses the mastery method you may have to take steps to help your child move the basics into long-term memory.

OUTCOME BASED EDUCATION

Outcome Based Education (OBE) goes a step further than mastery learning. The latter generally relates to specific goals, such as learning to multiply by three. OBE sets long-range goals, not just for academic achievement, but for the kind of student the school system will graduate. Theoretically, it is just as important for schools to produce a certain kind of student as one with acceptable achievement levels. This is another theory that makes one wonder about the ulterior motives of the education elite. A public school goal of producing a certain kind of person sounds more communistic than capitalistic.

In New York State, OBE came under the alias "A Compact for Learning." I had the dubious pleasure of attending an administrative-called meeting to gain faculty approval of our school's effort to establish its long-term goals. A committee had been guided through the development of the outcomes in the education jargon of the times. We eventually adopted the suggestions of the committee with few changes. The eight general statements were called exit outcomes and they are as follows:

Communicate and participate effectively with individuals, especially in a multicultural world. Use the tools of a modern technological society.

Demonstrate skills to manage successfully the various demands of everyday living.

Develop and demonstrate the skills to think critically, logically, and creatively: solve problems and develop attitudes that allow for individual initiative, cooperative effort, and lifelong learning.

Respect and practice basic civil values and acquire skills, knowledge, understanding, and attitudes necessary to participate in the world community.

Establish and maintain personal goals.

Recognize and appreciate unique gifts, talents, and interests of self and others.

Exercise personal, social, and moral responsibility, especially in dealing with wellness in individual health and in environmental issues.

To show you where this is all heading, I have extrapolated an outcome they did not quite dare to write:

Recognize the school district as the Great Omnipotent District (GOD) and be willing to dedicate their future children to GOD's wishes.

You might be interested in some observations I jotted down while attending the meeting. They will give you some real insight into the inter-workings of school district faculties.

It took forty-five minutes to make two rather simple decisions. If teacher X had not told teacher Y to "hush," it would have taken longer.

The committee strove for consensus (everyone agrees), but had to resort to rule by majority (more logical, but obviously not up to the new ideal).

Votes were all close, indicating a divided faculty.

The administration was absent from the meeting a great deal of the time. Perhaps they disliked sitting around in a meeting dominated by teachers, or thought they had more important things to do.

Some of the faculty relates to the verbalization of generalized goals. Others think it is a waste of time, but it has to be done, so they try to get it over with quickly.

Those, including myself, who considered it a waste of time, thought we should have been doing something that would be of mutual benefit. For instance, the school had a rule against students sitting on desks. Some teachers did not enforce the rule and sat on the desks themselves. You look like an ogre when you enforce a rule that other teachers ignore. We should have decided whether it was a good rule, and if it was, we should have agreed that everyone would enforce and obey that rule. If you take care of the little things, the big ones will take care of themselves.

Some faculty members think other members are a bunch of dummies and cannot wait to tell them how things should be done.

The aforementioned are thought of by other members as loud-mouthed, pushy individuals that in fact know a heck of a lot less then they think.

Some faculty members operate in a totally selfish mode.

The differences between elementary and secondary education are a built-in reason for faculty non-consensus.

WHAT DO TEACHERS REALLY THINK?

My notes from above indicate that teachers find it difficult to agree on anything. You would expect to hear of such dissension, but you don't. Most teachers are afraid that making waves will result in retaliation from school officials or their union. Consequently, most media releases concerning our schools come from school administrators, the education hierarchy, and the unions. Everyone should realize the things you hear and read about our schools do not reflect the views of all teachers. They may not even reflect the views of the majority.

Perhaps things have changed in the last couple of decades. Colleges may be more interested in producing a certain kind of teacher rather than one that is skilled. Unions strive to make teachers into demonstrators and propagandists. They tell them how to vote and use their money for political campaigning. Can a politically motivated teacher be an unbiased teacher? We expect fair presentation of both the pros and the cons of any controversial issue. The give and take of disagreement keeps things on an even keel in the classroom and in teacher meetings. It is a disservice to our nation if all teachers agree to agree.

TECHNOLOGY AND EDUCATION

Many education innovations are tied to advances in technology. Those in power tend to push the latest technology with little regard to its impact. Perhaps they think it makes them look good; perhaps there is money to be made and/or favors to be accumulated. Jumping in doesn't necessarily lead to good results. For instance, in the '60s, overhead projectors were the rage. There was several in our school, so I tried one, but I soon went back to chalk and the boards. When I retired in the '90s, a science teacher was the only teacher with an overhead projector.

In the '70s, public TV came to our rural area. Tall towers with flashing lights sprung up on various hilltops. The custodians erected antennas, strung wires, and soon every room had a TV set. All this time and money was spent so that the school could receive three major networks and a public TV channel. My students were already watching too much TV at home so I spent my time teaching them to use pencil, paper, and their minds. However, in the elementary wing, Sesame Street ran rampant. In some classes the TV sets flickered all morning, and then came the VCR so it could flicker all day.

The judicious use of TV may be acceptable, but schoolchildren should be spending the majority of their time involved in a conscious effort to learn. We do not hire teachers to sit their students if front of some entertaining information, hoping they will absorb some of it—we can hire baby-sitters to accomplish that.

Currently, we have computer programs and the Internet. Children may take to the computer like a duck to water, but computers should be limited as teaching tools at the elementary level. Like TV, they are entertaining and informative, but not nearly as focused as a well-managed class. Students need to be exposed to computers just as they are exposed to art, library, music, and physical education. However, it should be kept to a minimum—their basic education is much more important than their ability to use a computer that will be obsolete by the time they are in high school.

Early use of computers and other high tech devices leads to two big disadvantages, the lack of practice in penmanship and bad keyboarding habits. The formal keyboarding system that uses both hands and all your digits is obviously the best, but early users may develop their own one or two finger peck system.

The way we are going, children won't be able to do much of anything unless they have a computer or some other high tech device handy. Teachers who have their students spending a great deal of class time in front of them are letting the machine do the teaching. People—not machines—are the best teachers! If it were the other way around, teachers could be eliminated.

The Internet is a great way to gather current information, but you can also gather pornography and rip-off schemes. There are a host of outright lies and you can chat (send messages back and forth) with unknown people that may be liars, perverts, or criminals. Responsible use of the Internet is similar to the responsibilities of driving a car. Schools and parents should limit and closely monitor student use of this helpful but dangerous tool.

CLASS SIZE

You may not think of class size as an innovation, but the constant push toward smaller and smaller classes has certainly resulted in extreme change. Back in the '60s, it was nothing to see an elementary teacher with a class of thirty to forty students, perhaps with the part-time help of a teacher's aide. Recently in my school, a class of twenty-nine was split in two.

We are paying more and more to teachers to teach smaller and smaller classes. No wonder school taxes go up by leaps and bounds! School leaders attribute the necessity of smaller classes to the deterioration of the family, poor discipline at home, and a society so mobile the teacher must continually deal with student turnover. School officials don't want to admit it, but one of the biggest reasons for the reductions of class size is the deterioration of discipline within the schools.

Another contributing factor to smaller class size is "mainstreaming" or "inclusion." It places a child with a severe mental and/or physical handicap into a regular class. At one time these students were provided with a special program staffed with teachers that were trained to deal with them and their needs. Someone decided these children should go to regular classrooms.

They tried the plan in my school, which may be one of the reasons for splitting that class of twenty-nine. Even in small classes of fifteen, it must have been very difficult for the regular teachers to also function as special education teachers. These children have unusual needs and require individualized teaching plans. In one of our situations it caused havoc. The child could not adjust, would not behave, and greatly upset the whole class. The parents of this child—not the school administration—finally removed the child from the program because they could see that it was not working. The child left to a better circumstance and the remaining children had a better education environment.

The teachers' union constantly pressures for smaller and smaller classes. An increase in the number of teachers means more union dues can be collected. School administrators may not say so, but they actually favor smaller classes and more teachers because it broadens their power base. Most teachers are in favor of smaller classes, perhaps selfishly, but that is understandable. There are parents who believe smaller classes will help their children, so they also lobby for them. Board members, many of whom are parents, go along with the reduction of class size. The good news for parents is that their elementary child might attend a nice, neat, small class. The bad news is that small classes do not guarantee good education. We tend to lose sight of the fact that in an undisciplined class—with a poor teacher—half a dozen students are too many.

The theory that smaller classes provide a better education sounds very reasonable. However, my experience tells me a *disciplined* class of thirty students provides a better educational experience than a class of six. It is difficult to provide reasons. Perhaps the larger group asks more questions during class, maybe it is because there are more people to interact with, or it could be that the small class depends too much upon the teacher. We seem to have lost sight of the fact that in the long run, an ounce of student self-reliance is worth a pound of personal help. Your school should be able to provide your child with disciplined classes of more than twenty. If it can't, your school needs new management.

THE OPEN CLASSROOM

Over the last few decades, some of our schools have been busily tearing down walls and putting them up again. The reason behind all this construction and destruction is the "open classroom," where several classes meet in a large open area. The theory is that this would facilitate the flow of teachers, students, and ideas back and forth throughout the school.

One rationalization used for the open classroom is that since you are apt to work in a hubbub, you should learn in one. One flaw with this argument is that if students learn to tune out the noise from the adjoining class, they may also tune out the teacher. Although learning can take place in this atmosphere, it hinders more than it helps. It is tough enough to keep a child's attention in a closed classroom. Just try it when the sounds and movements of the other classes are ever-present. It is one thing to ask a mature person to work in a noisy environment; it is another thing to ask an elementary student to learn the basics under such conditions. Students, particularly at the elementary level, should be provided with the best possible environment for learning.

Some educators point to existing open classrooms that are effective, but if you put these same teachers and students into rooms, the results would be even better. Once something like the open classroom gets started in education, you just can't seem to get rid of it—new administrators keep rediscovering it, often to the detriment of the entire school system. My oldest granddaughter was in an elementary open classroom for a couple of years, and she complained about the distractions. I observed that her teachers were themselves distracted by the other classes because they build walls out of filing cabinets, shelves, and television sets to make their area as private as possible. This one looming physical fact should be enough to make school officials question the advisability of open classrooms.

THE DAILY SCHEDULE

Other innovations relate to such commonplace aspects as the day's routine. In middle school and high school, students move from class to class and are taught by specialists in all fields. Traditionally, core subjects meet in forty-minute classes every school day. This is one of the things administrators like to keep changing. They change the length of the class, they change the number of periods per day, and they come up with class schedules that change every other day or every day for five days. One wonders if these changes in the school day are made to facilitate learning or just to give the administrators something to do.

My oldest granddaughter left her elementary open classroom to enter middle school and its brand new schedule. Following is how it appeared in the monthly school newsletter.

Sixth Grade	
A Day	**B Day**
Block 1 8:10—9:23	Block 5 8:10—9:23
Music Block 9:25—10:05	
Block 2 10:07—11:20	Block 6 10:07—11:20
Lunch 11:22—11:58	
Block 3 12:00—1:12	Block 7 12:00—1:12
Block 4 1:14—2:24	Block 8 1:14—2:24

1. Language Arts (every day)
2. Language Arts (every day)
3. Math
4. Science

5. Social Studies

6. Physical Education

7. Exploratory: (Art, Health, Technology, Home & Career Skills)

8. Music Experience: (Band, Orchestra, Choir, or General Music)

Does it look confusing? It did to me. The first thing I noticed was that the course numbers did not match up with the block numbers, or language arts would meet twice in one day rather than every day. My granddaughter informed me that if your renumber the classes 4, 6, 2, 5, 1, 3 7, 8, you can then tell when she was scheduled for each subject.

It also seemed like a magnate school for music with a forty-minute class every day, plus a seventy-minute block every other day. Students could participate in band or chorus during the forty-minute music period scheduled every day, but if they did not, they had study hall. The number eight block is a kind of activity period primarily taken up with what is called team time, which probably is used to combine the efforts of the various music groups or to introduce more education innovation.

My college classes did not meet every day, but at least a given class always met on a given day of the week. Every Monday my granddaughter had to figure out if it was an A or a B day. Actually, it was probably easier for her than her teachers to keep things straight. The following were listed in the newsletter as advantages to the new format (following the * is my interpretation):

Increased useable instruction time.

* This is not true! If thirty minutes are allowed for lunch and two minutes for passing, an eight period class schedule with forty-one minute classes is possible in the same time frame. That is 205 minutes per week while the length of the average block (seventy-two minutes) times two and a half is only 180 minutes a week. The every day schedule provides 15 more hours per year. I would think an eight-period schedule plus lunch would be adequate for middle school. If it's not the school is robbing time from the core subjects to spend it on this or that.

Teaching with a variety of instructional Models is encouraged

* Teachers will have to resort to a big bag of tricks to keep eleven-year-olds interested and busy in the same subject for seventy minutes.

Instructional strategies that consider the characteristics of the adolescent learner are emphasized.

* They play games.

Ability to plan extended lessons.

* This is too long for most young minds. It would be too long for me!

Number of class changes and transition time is reduced.

* This means more in-class breaks and wasted in-class time.

Interdisciplinary instruction is easier to facilitate and teams can reorganize blocks of time for group instructional activities.

* Teachers are pressured into spending more and more time on innovative projects and less and less time on teaching the basics.

More minutes for planning.

* More free time for teachers.

Work missed because of absence is easier to gather and monitor.

* Why? If a student misses one day in a regular schedule, they will see the teacher the day they return. This may not happen in an every-other-day schedule.

Fewer assignments, quizzes and tests on any given day for students.

* Is that good?

Teachers prepare for fewer courses each day.

* A knowledgeable teacher, provided with good supplies, does not need a great deal of preparation time.

More passing time between classes.

* The less time students spend in the hall the better.

Elimination of most study halls.

* Well-run study halls are a plus, not a minus.

Perhaps, I am too critical. Perhaps, we should all be more critical and not passively accept everything forced upon us by the education elite. The best part of the new schedule was that my granddaughter spent double time on language arts, but unfortunately that only lasted one year.

It seems to me that math teachers would be very upset. A block of seventy-three minutes every other day is not the way to teach math. Students cannot digest a great deal of math at one sitting; they need the constant reinforcement of an everyday class. Weekends and holidays are going to cause such long time spans between math classes that some students will forget almost as much as they have learned. The longer blocks are preferable for courses such as art, music, technology, and physical education, where students spend much of a traditional class period getting ready and cleaning up. Are those courses more important than the basics?

LET'S CHANGE THE SCHEDULE FOR TEACHERS

Why do all the teachers of a school have to work the same hours? A traditional everyday schedule in the morning for the academic courses and the new longer blocks in the afternoon could benefit all subjects. For instance, an everyday math class as short as thirty minutes, supplemented by a long math lab every Thursday afternoon, would be a great way to teach math. The math lab would be an independent study situation where students that had fallen behind could catch up, while other students could delve into some non-curriculum mathematics. The academic teachers could come to school early, take care of the morning chores such as homeroom, teach their classes, have their labs, do their preparations, and leave early. The teachers of cultural subjects such as art, music, technology, and physical education could come in later, do their preparations, teach their classes, take care of the afternoon chores, and go home later. This schedule would give emphasis to the academic subjects, afford the cultural subjects increased teaching time, and provide the students with a more flexible program.

CHANGE FOR THE SAKE OF CHANGE

The first big detrimental change in public school teaching I encountered was called "modern math." In the early '60s some major changes were made in high school math and they blossomed into major changes throughout the public school system. They even changed the procedures and concepts covered in basic elementary arithmetic. Young children came home from school spouting words their parents had never heard and doing arithmetic in ways they had never seen. They were not really new ways; there are not many new things in arithmetic. They were not really better ways; we were already using the best ways. They were just different! Education leaders were more interested in getting in on the bandwagon of big change than checking the effectiveness of these transformations.

The failure of modern math and other education innovations hasn't taught our public school hierarchy a thing. Students and their teachers still face an endless chain of fads and trends engineered by our academia that try to make a name for themselves—and usurp more education dollars—by promoting innovation. These unproved changes are forced on our schools by naive state legislators and unfit administrators, often to the dismay of the teachers and to the detriment of the students. It is a crime when school officials change something good into something bad and suffer no consequences. They simply keep changing—sometimes back to the way it was—and have the nerve to expect commendation for their accomplishments.

It seems our education elite are either misguided opportunists, changing things for the sake of change, or they have a hidden agenda. Group study, cooperative education, and homogeneous grouping promote comradeship, which is related to communism. Traditional study promotes individualism, which is one of the basic values of our land. We expect our schools to promote these values. If they are purposely trying to tear them down, we must take action.

It is obvious that changes in education are coming from the wrong places. We need professional teachers working directly with school boards and parents to provide good schools. Forced changes from the top down are apt to do more harm than good. Every school is unique and the one-solution-fits-all can't work. Those closest to the work and the problems are in the best position to make appropriate changes. We should force the education elite and the unions to release their stranglehold on our schools. However, it will be more difficult to change the education establishment than the classroom, but it could be done. We need school boards that will fight for independence and politicians that are willing to grant their wishes. We need many involved parents that will support their efforts.

ACKNOWLEDGMENTS

The cover girl is Sydney Goodsell my middle granddaughter. Her mother Gina and her father Eric provided support and comments. My oldest granddaughter Ashley and her mother Georgia were proofreaders.

Thanks to Lee Martin, Constance Synakowski and Marybeth Thompsett, fellow public school educators and contributors.

Photo of Sydney Goodsell by Eric Goodsell

Photo of Donald Goodsell by Georgia Goodsell Martin

www.ingramcontent.com/pod-product-compliance
Lightning Source LLC
Chambersburg PA
CBHW071517040426
42444CB00008B/1681